THE DIGITAL PR PLAYBOOK

About JBH

Launched in 2013 by three friends and colleagues, JBH is a digital PR and SEO agency with offices in Manchester and London.

Our award-winning team has built a reputation for delivering outstanding results for brands around the world. Our unique blend of SEO strategy, on-page performance, and digital PR campaigns consistently generates results with measurable impact that line up with important commercial goals.

We're experts at earning highly relevant and authoritative backlinks that, when combined with effective on-page and technical SEO strategies, have been proven to boost organic visibility and build brand fame.

What others think

"This guide offers a comprehensive and actionable approach to digital PR, covering both strategic foundations and practical tactics. It provides a broad context for understanding why digital PR is essential for driving organic growth and increasing brand awareness. It also details how to effectively execute a digital PR strategy, making it an invaluable resource for anyone aiming to enhance their digital PR efforts."

- Beth Nunnington, VP of Global Digital PR, Journey Further.

"If you have been seeking a resource that tells you everything you need to know about building links for SEO with digital PR, look no further. This book has everything from the history to results and best practices on how to use digital PR to drive growth for your business. Once I started reading, I could not put it down!"

- Eli Schwartz, author of Product-Led SEO and Growth Consultant.

*"The Digital PR Playbook offers a timely and comprehensive exploration of the evolving digital landscape where public relations meets search engine optimisation. It emphasises the

importance of quality, relevance and ethical practices in digital public relations.

The JBH team tells the story of the transition from rudimentary link-building to the practice of planning, creativity, content, engagement and measurement, providing a framework for modern digital public relations practice. The book provides practical tips, case studies and expert insights on effective digital PR strategies, keeping you informed and up-to-date in this rapidly changing field.

The book is a comprehensive resource for marketers, SEO professionals, and public relations practitioners who want to leverage digital public relations techniques to improve online visibility, brand awareness and business growth."

- Stephen Waddington, Director, Wadds Inc.

Contents

Introduction

Written by: Jane Hunt

It feels like a critical time in digital PR, so essentially, it felt like the perfect time to write this book. Some agencies are closing their digital PR departments, interest in AI and how tech and innovation could transform the search experience has increased, and TikTok search is threatening *Google's* patch. So, it's a really interesting (and challenging) time to be running a digital PR agency.

I was asked on a podcast the other day if I thought AI and *Google's* AI-powered search experience (SGE), would end digital PR and link building as we currently know it. However, I rightly (or wrongly) don't think organic search and the role of backlinks can be dismantled that quickly. Plus, with *Google's* focus on the quality of content and its recent *link spam* update, I actually believe that this is the time for digital PR to flourish and why this book is necessary now.

Why Write a Book About Digital PR?

This is something we've been discussing at JBH for a while and finally, we just thought we'd get it done and get it out there. Partly because many brands lack an understanding of what digital PR is and what it can achieve, and can also be put off by the initial investment, which, unlike PPC, might not provide an immediate ROI.

It's also apparent that many brands don't understand how it can be used and that it has multiple marketing benefits, a few of which are:

- Improving search rankings and increasing organic traffic.
- Building brand awareness and credibility.
- Impacting commercial objectives like enquiries and sales.

Secondly, there's a lot of confusion about how to do it properly! So, this book aims to also bust some myths, and provide advice and expertise that can be immediately applied in any organisation.

Why Is JBH Qualified to Write It?

Having been delivering digital PR campaigns in one form or another for the last ten years, it's fair to say we've seen and tried everything. We've worked with B2B and B2C brands, some huge and some small, across an array of industries. This includes brands in personal finance, healthcare, property, and FMCG — and we've delivered hundreds of campaigns and built thousands of links for them.

Over the years, the SEO industry and link building as a tactic has changed dramatically. We started off creating fun infographics and interactive content, and now we deliver data-led campaigns that position our clients as thought leaders, put them on the map, and can even impact change. Like most channels and activities, link building matured and digital PR emerged as the more professional, considered, and credible approach to link building that not only builds organic visibility, but also builds brands.

Plus, we've hired some of the best talent in the industry, from SEO and content to data, design, and traditional PR experts. This ensures we have the whole process covered, from digital PR strategy, ideation, content creation, to outreach, and reporting.

Lastly, because I believe JBH are pioneers. We don't just accept the norm, the way things have been done, we're constantly trying to improve and innovate.

"Digital PR is challenging — many agencies offer it, but few do it well."

We're now in a time when agencies and in-house teams need to be able to demonstrate the value of digital PR, beyond a quantity of links. So that's what we're doing, working on new methods to measure, analyse, and report on the value digital PR can offer brands. Because this industry keeps growing and adapting, your tactics should not remain static, but evolve and hopefully thrive.

Who Is This Book For?

Anyone who is...

- Already working in digital PR but wants to enhance their knowledge.
- In-house and wants a better understanding of how an agency goes about delivering digital PR campaigns and the tactics we use.
- Working in a digital marketing role and wants to find out where digital PR can fit in and complement other channel objectives.
- Interested in strategy and techniques for building links to category and product pages.
- Looking for ways to measure and evaluate digital PR performance that goes beyond reporting on the quantity of links.
- A business owner who wants to understand the benefits and how it can impact organic traffic, build trust, and increase the frequency and quality of enquiries and sales.
- Open-minded and able to see that there are more ways than one to build relevant and authoritative links.

Who Is This Book NOT For?

Anyone who...

- Thinks digital PR is a quick win — it's not, it's an investment, but one that DOES pay off if you're patient.
- Normally buys links — it's not our style, we prefer to earn them the traditional PR way!
- Doesn't want ideas and strategies on how to improve the performance of their digital PR campaigns.
- Thinks they know it all already. We're always learning and tweaking, so I'm sure there'll be a revised edition of this book in a few years!

So the Big Question Is... What Is Digital PR?

Rather than pull a definition from *Google*, I'm providing my interpretation, that we've built our service offering around.

"Digital PR is the intersection of traditional PR, content marketing, and SEO. We're borrowing from traditional PR and content marketing techniques, and fusing them with SEO strategy to build organic search visibility AND drive brand credibility and trust.

— **Jane Hunt CEO**

Let me break it down a bit more...

First comes the SEO strategy — What the objectives are, how we will approach them, and how the strategy will dictate how we deliver campaigns and measure success. Digital PR, also known as 'link building' and 'online PR', was born from the need to build links in SEO, as backlinks are a ranking factor by search engines like *Google*.

Ten years ago, when JBH first started building links, SEOs were primarily concerned with building several backlinks. However, there was still the desire to get links from top-tier online publications like *Mashable*, *The Guardian*, and *HuffPost*. We were creating either entertaining or data-led infographics and interactive experiences, that journalists could embed with (hopefully) a link back to our client's site (usually their blog where the content sat, or the homepage).

But over the years, this practice has evolved from this type of link building to one that is more holistic, and more mature. We're now also considering the brand and how we can use content to not only build links, but also build awareness and credibility with target audiences.

Chapter 1: The Need

1.1 The Difference Between Digital PR and Traditional PR

Written by: James Renhard

Before we dive into the world of digital PR, we have to answer one major question — What is the difference between digital PR and traditional PR? As our industry becomes more prevalent around the globe, a question that's being asked with increasing frequency, is about the differences between digital PR and its more traditional counterpart; PR.

What's the Best? What's the Most Effective? Which One Is Best for My Business?

To give a clear answer to the differences between traditional PR and digital PR, it's maybe best to start by explaining the similarities. Both traditional PR and digital PR can be employed to manage a brand's reputation, and speak to a demographic that the brand wants to target — be that an audience they already have, or one that they're looking to reach.

Traditional PR

Generally speaking, yes, we are painting with somewhat of a broad brush here, but that broad brush will be applied throughout. Traditional PR relies on offline media, such as print, radio, TV, events, and sometimes product testing to speak to an intended audience. At its most basic, the goal of traditional PR is brand fame and/or awareness, via placements within offline media in the form of an interview, commentary, or segment feature.

Digital PR

This form of digital PR is much more heavily focused on online media (brace yourself for a caveat) such as websites and social channels to engage with the audience. At its most basic, the goal of digital PR is SEO, and helping people search for a brand, a page on the website, or even a specific product when searching online, via earning links from other websites.

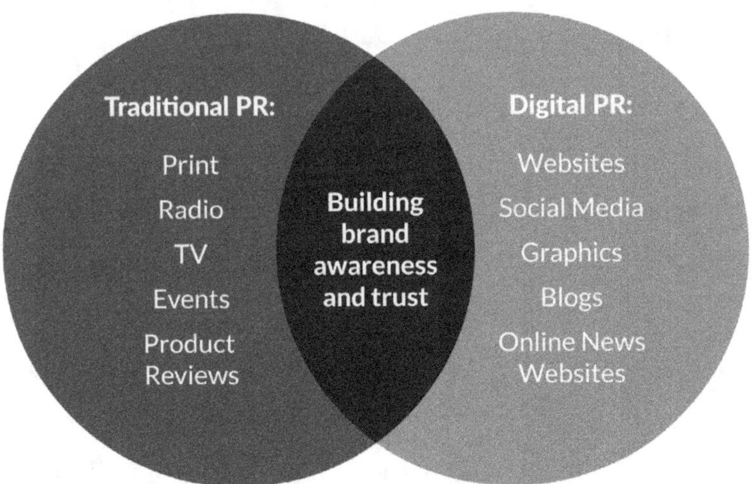

However, and here's that caveat I mentioned — as a by-product of digital PR, we often see an increase in brand fame **as well.**

Although the goal is to earn links, there are often many unlinked placements within media, along with increased broadcast opportunities, all of which boost brand awareness and consideration among an engaged audience. Furthermore, digital PRs will regularly employ tactics and approaches borrowed, such as feature pitching. This includes targeting specific articles, usually weighty, long-form, thought-leadership pieces, to a specific journalist at a specific publication.

Looking in a little more detail, here are some of the key attributes of digital PR, that highlight the ways it differs from the more traditional variant...

Measurable Results

Closely aligned with SEO (more on this later), digital PR provides instant and detailed metrics with which success can be measured. *Google* ranking equivalency scores (domain authority and domain rating), market share indicators (share of search), and bespoke, in-house metrics like (search impact and brand impact), can be applied to the results achieved by digital PR — immediately indicating the impact of a link or placement on a domain. Access to these metrics allows brands using digital PR to quantify the impact of their efforts and adjust strategies accordingly, making their approach incredibly dynamic.

A Targeted Approach, With Wider Reach

Digital PR allows for very specific targeting, in turn, allowing brands to reach specific audiences and demographics. Sometimes in very niche sectors that traditional PR struggles to reach, or simply does not know about. This significantly increases the value of digital PR campaigns, as it ensures more of the people who are likely to be customers can be reached, and with the right message.

But, at the same time, digital PR can be truly global, quickly reaching regions, countries, and cultures with the click of a button. Without hefty investment, traditional PR can struggle to reach these corners of the globe, and even when it does, it tends to do so much more slowly.

A Dynamic Approach

Digital PR allows brands to respond swiftly to breaking news, emerging trends, events, and even crises, maintaining a timely and relevant presence in the digital landscape. It's not uncommon for media around breaking news to be led, or sometimes even driven, by comments and reactions from digital PR sources. This agility, which is not easily recreated through traditional PR tactics, also applies to events in pop culture, and emerging trends from social media. Brands with a solid and flexible digital PR strategy are always ready and able to be at the start of key conversations among the audience they want to reach.

SEO Benefits

Arguably, the most significant difference between digital PR and the more traditional form is the significant impact it can have on a brand's SEO efforts. The links earned from digital PR activity will significantly boost the visibility of a domain on search engines such as *Google*. It will make the brand, its products, and the expertise it can offer, easier to find for customers when they're searching online — which, in turn, dramatically boosts conversion, supporting a brand's commercial goals.

Google's own Senior Search Analyst, John Mueller (a sort of Demi-God among the SEO community), tweeted that digital PR is...

"Just as critical as tech SEO, probably more so, in many cases."

Now, before I have a line of traditional PRs waiting for me outside the office doors, this is not to say traditional PR is not working, and shouldn't be something brands consider. It's a $107 billion industry and hasn't got there accidentally. My goal here has been to highlight some key attributes of digital PR, as a way to create greater clarity between the younger, more emerging industry, and it's more established sibling.

1.2 Why Do Brands Need Digital PR?

Written by: Jane Hunt

In the last chapter, exploring the differences between digital PR and traditional PR, we touched on the benefits that digital PR can have on organic search visibility, as well as building brand awareness and driving credibility and trust. But now we're going to talk about why digital PR is such an important part of the marketing mix.

We like to think that digital PR is a much more modern and sophisticated way of building backlinks for brands. Just to provide some history, digital PR was born from link building, including earned, paid private blog networks, and guest posting tactics.

However, over the years, we've called the tactic of editorially-earned links digital PR, because we're not just building links, we're earning PR coverage, building brand awareness, and driving credibility — to name a few benefits. It's those backlinks that make digital PR a fundamental part of SEO. Backlinks have long been considered a major ranking signal by search engines when analysing the strength of a website, and where to position the website in the SERPs to match a user's search query.

There are many key ranking 'signals' or 'factors' that search engines like *Google* consider, but a few of the most important are:

- **The Quality and Freshness of On-Page Content:** *Google's* recent E.E.A.T guidelines (experience, expertise, authority, and trustworthiness), which aim to improve user experience and decrease misinformation, are now considered key ranking signals.
- **Page Experience:** This is made up of multiple signals, but looks to reward pages that have been created with the user in mind first and foremost. For example, fast load times, useful content, easy to read, and mobile friendly with Core Web Vitals metrics in mind.
- **Links:** While they have long been ranking factors, their importance has grown considerably over the years, with search engines like *Google* looking more closely at the quality and relevance of those links, rather than just quantity. *Google* rewards editorially earned links, but has penalised many websites with 'spammy' links over the years.

So, this is where the **need** for backlinks comes from — they are an important ranking factor for search engines like *Google*. John Mueller, at an SEO conference in 2023, said

"Digital PR was fantastic, but the need for links is growing".

With digital PR experiencing a sizeable boom, more and more brands are seeing the value of digital PR, not just for gaining increased visibility and rankings, but for the other benefits it offers highlighted in the previous chapter. However, as more brands invest in digital PR, it can become even more of a challenge for brands to make their mark in highly competitive marketplaces.

This is why you must have a solid digital PR strategy that aligns closely with the SEO objectives and wider marketing and business goals. Nowadays, any agency can build backlinks, but can they build links that are going to have a measurable, visible impact in search, support brand objectives, **and** provide commercial value too?

Chapter 2: The History of Link Building

2.1 Digital PR vs Link Building

Written by: Rebecca Moss

In the quest to elevate a brand's online presence, the battleground lies within the intricate realm of search engine results pages (SERPs). A fundamental strategy for achieving dominance in these results, is SEO, the craft of refining online content to ascend the ranks of *Google's* first page.

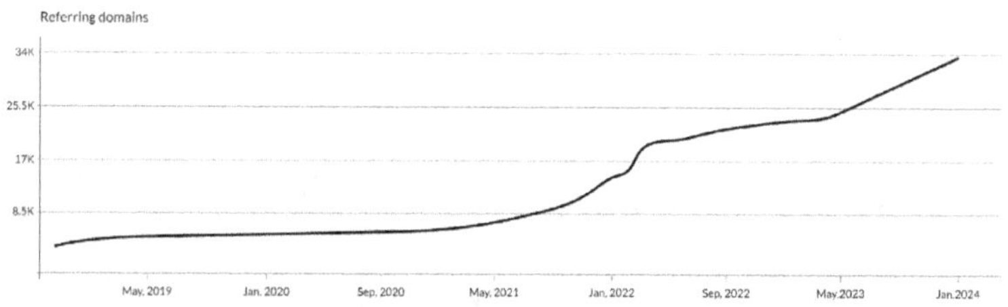

Google and Link Building

In SEO, link building or link earning, emerges as a crucial method. If SEO is the theoretical foundation of *Google* rankings, then earning quality backlinks is the practical implementation. In essence, this involves securing links from authoritative, relevant, and powerful websites, both large and niche. The significance lies in *Google* 'crawling' the content on these websites, finding these links, and attributing them as a vote of quality, relevance, experience, and assurance back to your website.

Search engine optimisation professionals strategically leverage thorough and ongoing keyword research to identify areas where website performance is lacking. This highly technical process always circles back to the brand and the authority it holds in its niche.

For instance, the person responsible for earning backlinks for an air conditioning company, will craft content focused on topics likely to be searched by individuals seeking cooling solutions. This content will incorporate short-tail keywords such as 'air conditioning repair,' 'air-con,' 'heating and cooling,' or region-specific terms like 'HVAC' and 'AC' for the US market. And more specific long-tail search queries such as 'How much will an air con unit cost to run each month?'.

Beyond Link Building

Link Building is often confused with digital PR with the terms being used interchangeably, however, I would argue they are completely different disciplines. While link building and digital PR are somewhat interconnected, the latter extends its reach beyond the former.

Digital PR operates at a higher level, striving not only to secure relevant links, but build brand fame, earn trust, showcase thought leadership, and spark meaningful conversations. Digital PR kicks off with extensive research, transcending traditional keyword exploration. The focus shifts to people and their emotional engagement. It employs tactics such as impactful statistics, interactive content, and compelling stories around newsworthy topics, to resonate with the audience on a deeper level.

Beyond connecting the brand to the customer, digital PR also establishes connections with journalists. By providing intriguing angles or 'hooks', digital PR professionals foster relationships that entice journalists to return for more content. These relationships, built on mutual benefit, facilitate the seamless acquisition of features for clients in the future.

Results and Reporting

As the pursuit of boosting brand awareness aligns with the scientific precision of reporting, the paths of digital PR and link building converge. Despite their differing approaches, both practices share a common goal — generating links to enhance website authority and search engine visibility.

For link builders, the primary objective is catching the attention of *Google*, aiming for a higher rank, and toppling competitors from the coveted first-page spot. Digital PR, on the other hand, delves deeper. While impressing *Google* remains paramount, the focus extends to impressing people. It focuses on creating content that not only captures attention but also sparks conversations, empowering digital PR campaigns to boost rankings and leave a lasting impact.

Intriguingly, meticulously crafted digital PR campaigns often garner attention from journalists repeatedly. Furthermore, if backed by a robust dataset, the content becomes a versatile asset, ready to be repackaged and repurposed for future campaigns.

A Deeper Dive Into Link Building

A link builder's toolkit is replete with tools and techniques honed to perfection, all with the singular objective of climbing *Google's* rankings. Keyword research is the foundation of link building, steering the strategy in a way that makes commercial sense for the brand. Link builders meticulously analyse keyword performance to identify areas where a website is lagging, they also look for gaps and opportunities in competitors' strategies for 'quick win' keyword ranking opportunities.

These insights guide the creation of targeted content that aligns with user queries, ensuring the brand remains visible to its intended audience. Furthermore, the contextual relevance of link placement is paramount. A link from a reputable source within the same industry carries more weight in the eyes of search engines. The intricate dance between keywords, content, and authoritative links, forms the backbone of link building, driving the website towards the summit of SERPs.

Crafting Engaging Narratives

While link building is rooted in technical precision, digital PR takes a more holistic approach. It goes beyond the confines of keyword research and seeks to craft narratives that resonate with audiences on a profound level. Digital PR professionals are similar to storytellers, creating compelling stories that not only capture attention but also evoke emotions. Research in digital PR extends beyond traditional keyword analysis. It delves into the psyche of the target audience, seeking to understand their preferences, concerns, and aspirations. Armed with this deep understanding, digital PR campaigns are designed to strike a chord with the audience, leaving an indelible impression.

The Power of Relationships in Digital PR

In the realm of digital PR, relationships are currency. Building connections with journalists is not merely a means to an end, but an ongoing process that yields lasting benefits. Journalists are the gatekeepers to media visibility, and digital PR professionals understand the importance of cultivating and nurturing these relationships on an ongoing basis.

Providing journalists with unique angles, exclusive data, and captivating stories, positions the brand that the digital PR professional represents as a valuable and trusted resource. As journalists find reliability in the content provided by digital PR professionals, a symbiotic relationship forms. This mutual trust makes it easier to secure features, interviews, and coverage for clients, creating a ripple effect that enhances the brand's online presence.

Digital PR Beyond Google

While both link building and digital PR share the goal of impressing *Google*, digital PR extends its reach to impress people beyond the algorithms. Crafting content that goes beyond mere visibility, digital PR campaigns seek to make a lasting impact on the audience. The content created in a digital PR campaign often transcends its initial purpose.

Well-thought-out campaigns, backed by robust datasets and compelling narratives, have the potential to be picked up by journalists repeatedly. This not only amplifies the brand's visibility but also positions it as a thought leader in its industry.

Repackaging and Repurposing

One of the distinguishing features of a successful digital PR campaign is its longevity. Unlike link building — where the focus is primarily on securing links to climb *Google's* rankings — digital PR campaigns have the power to endure beyond their initial launch.

Content generated in a digital PR campaign, especially when supported by a strong dataset, can be repackaged and repurposed for future campaigns. This versatility adds value to the content, ensuring that the brand's message continues to resonate with the audience over time. A well-crafted narrative becomes an asset that keeps on giving, contributing to the brand's sustained online visibility.

Chapter 3: Backlink Architecture

3.1 What Are the Different Types of Backlinks?

Written by: Rebecca Moss

A backlink *(a link, hyperlink)* is a link created when one website links to another. To search engines like *Google*, it's typically seen as an endorsement of the content on the linked site, from the linking site. To human users, it's a bridge between one page and another, typically offering further, more in-depth, or additional information or resources around the topic of the page they're reading. A deep dive into the links pointing towards your domain is essential for a digital PR strategy.

The right links in the right places can help boost referral traffic and rankings for your key terms. No purchased link can compete with the power of links earned via a successful digital PR campaign.

When done right, it's a marketing technique that can bring those all-important relevant backlinks, as well as social media shares, referral traffic, and coverage, and will build your brand along with your traffic.

There are, first and foremost, a few things to look at that concern the link itself...

Relevance

A high domain rating and domain authority are great, but you also want your links to be topically relevant. With topical relevance comes the target market and language. That does not mean that links from foreign websites are not good, but they should be relevant to your brand and the content you publish.

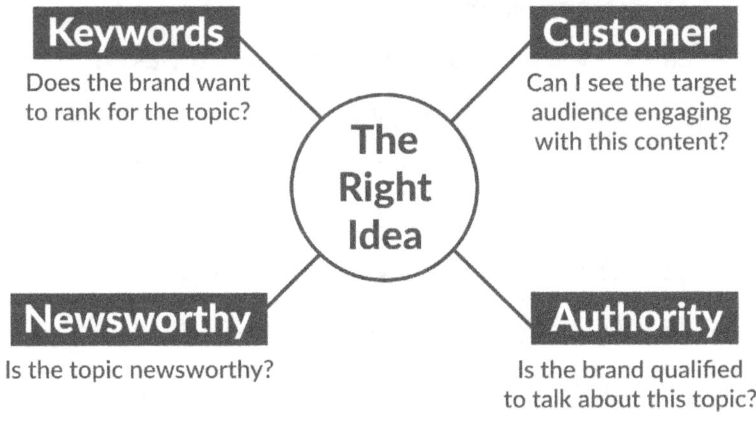

Link Type

- **Content Links:** Links can come in many shapes and forms, but the one we strive for is a link in content. For this, it is important how a link is embedded. Does it seem natural? Is it relevant? Does it make sense that this journalist is mentioning your brand in that context and not a competitor? If the answers to those questions is no, then the link might give the impression of a paid link that has been shoehorned in by a not-so-clever link builder.

- **Image Links:** Another type of link that can be good is an image link. However, a high number of image links in a backlink profile can also be an indicator of spam.

- **Sitewide Links or Links in the Navigation:** These are nice if you want to connect your different brands. The value they bring for SEO, though, is disputed, as it can be easily manipulated.

- **Links in User Comments or Directories:** The same applies here — if you can easily access a forum or a comment section or submit links in a directory, the value for SEO is low. Those tactics worked in the past, but *Google's* algorithm has evolved over time. If it is too easy, it probably does not make a big impact.

Follow vs Nofollow

Google has changed its stance on nofollow Links plenty of times. They now seem to hold more value than they used to, but a follow link is still preferred in the industry. Links marked as 'sponsored' hold the least value but can still get you some brand exposure. Keep in mind that a natural backlink profile always has a certain percentage of all link types. If a profile looks 'too clean', it probably is. The link itself is a nice achievement, but when it comes to measuring value, it is also important to look at the rest of the website.

Traffic

Is this website getting traffic? Is it ranking for a significant number of keywords? Do both numbers align? If a website ranks for 500 keywords, but the traffic estimate is only 20 visitors per month, the value of the website is questionable. You also want to take penalties into account.

A website can have a high traffic flow (TF) but have been penalised by the search engine. Traffic and ranking drops are good indicators to recognise a penalised site.

Syndication

It is no secret that duplicate content is not good for SEO, and yet, syndication is an acknowledged tactic. Where duplication ends and syndication starts can be hard to determine at times. When it comes to outreach campaigns, one journalist might publish your story and others re-publish what the first one wrote.

That can significantly increase the number of links to your campaign. When measuring their value, though, the first link is a lot more important than the syndicated links.

Paid Links

We may sound like a broken record, but buying links is not a recommended way to do SEO. Yet, we still see many websites and brands doing it. This can also impact your outreach campaigns. You might have earned the link without any payment in return, but if that same website is also selling links, your link might get devalued too. This aspect is hard to measure, as neither we nor *Google's* algorithm could ever determine for sure whether a link was paid for or not. But if it looks like a duck, swims like a duck, and quacks like a duck, then it probably is a duck. Try to avoid those websites in the first place.

Is the URL Indexed?

This last one seems to be the most obvious, but is still forgotten regularly. If the URL of the page that is linking to you is not indexed in *Google*, the link cannot pass any value. Simple as that. The link should not only be devalued in your reporting, but it should also not be counted towards your KPIs until it is indexed.

What Matters to the Journalist?

When we do an outreach campaign for digital PR, we are primarily trying to reach journalists — those who can pick up our content and publish new content around it with a link. In that context, we should also look at those metrics that matter to journalists. Among those, we find the number of page views, the time spent on the page, comment activity, and social shares — in short, engagement metrics. Those figures do not have a direct impact on rankings, but they increase your chances of attracting links significantly. Additionally, it provides brand exposure.

Counting links and noting DA or DR figures remain the most feasible ways to measure the success of a backlink campaign, but there is more to take into account in your reports and campaign creation. Most importantly, one single link is not tipping the scale — it is your overall backlink profile that matters.

What Are Toxic Backlinks?

Not all backlinks are equal, and just because you didn't build anything dodgy doesn't mean they aren't there. Toxic backlinks can potentially damage your SEO efforts, meaning lower rankings and less traffic. When building links to a domain that is new to you, it's always good to ask if any link work has been done before – and what kind. *Google* cracked down hard on backlinks that attempted to manipulate rankings back in 2012, so if any link work was carried out before then, the chances are it could be toxic.

Way back when SEO became a popular digital marketing tool, the backlink scene was more wild west than World Wide Web. Link builders could build blog networks and direct thousands of backlinks to their domain within minutes, or even rent link space on high-powered sites to give themselves a boost.

This worked, and it worked too well. In 2012, *Google* introduced their *Penguin* update, which all but put an end to this behaviour and sought to level the playing field, so more money didn't mean high rankings. It also puts its users first, ranking sites based on the quality of its backlinks rather than just the quantity.

Where Do Toxic Backlinks Come From?

Historic black hat link building is a big cause of low-quality links, but there are other routes for these links to come pointing to your domain. Yet toxic link building isn't always historic, and many still rely on these techniques to boost rankings. While the days of buying backlinks, PBNs (private blog networks), and expensive guest posts should be long gone, there are still plenty of domains reaping the benefits of bad linking. However, this is a ticking time bomb and frankly – your site deserves better.

A natural backlink profile is made up of links on domains that are relevant, good quality, and earned, not bought. When doing some domain digging, it's important to stay curious and always be on the lookout for something that could be harmful, but don't jump to conclusions. Often there is an honest explanation for any dodgy links, the most essential thing is to ensure your domain stays safe. *Google* has become really good at ignoring spammy links, and if it finds any, its AI will ignore and devalue them.

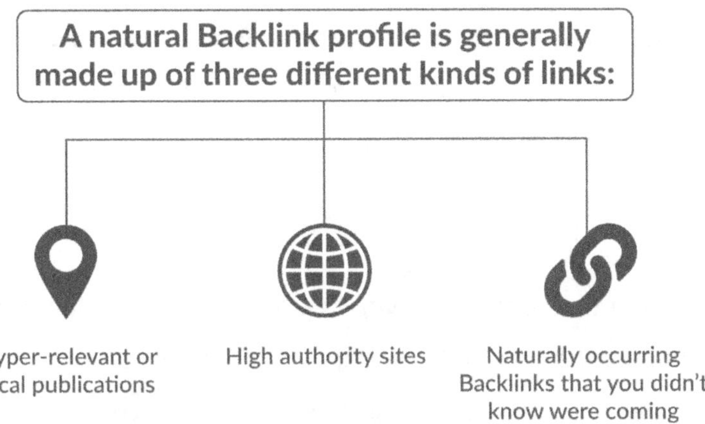

Sometimes *Google* can penalise your site if it detects a large number of unnatural or spammy links. In such circumstances, you can submit a disavow file to *Google* and ask them to ignore those links. This tactic is an old one and would only need to be used on rare occasions.

3.2 The Steps to a Successful Backlink Campaign

Written by: Rebecca Moss

There are two things in the digital world that can make or break an online business — content and links. If you have a business with a website that already attracts users, you probably know about the content side of things. After all, that is what helps customers find your website, engage with it, and eventually make a purchase, sign up for a newsletter, or support your cause (or whatever else you want them to do). But what about those links? How many backlinks does your website have? And more importantly: How many of those links are legit and well-deserved? This is where link building becomes relevant.

Link Building via Digital PR Campaigns

While the content on your website is entirely in your own hands, the link building depends on many external factors that you cannot always influence — or can you? In the early days of the internet and SEO, you could simply pay somebody to link to your website. But the rules have changed, and paid link building is not only losing its impact, but can also lead to search engine penalties and destroy all SEO efforts you have made over the years. Therefore, that is not a viable option. So, what is? The answer is simple:

digital PR and backlink campaigns! Before you get on the job, though, it is important to understand what makes a successful backlink campaign and how to create one.

Let us break this down into five steps that lead to links...

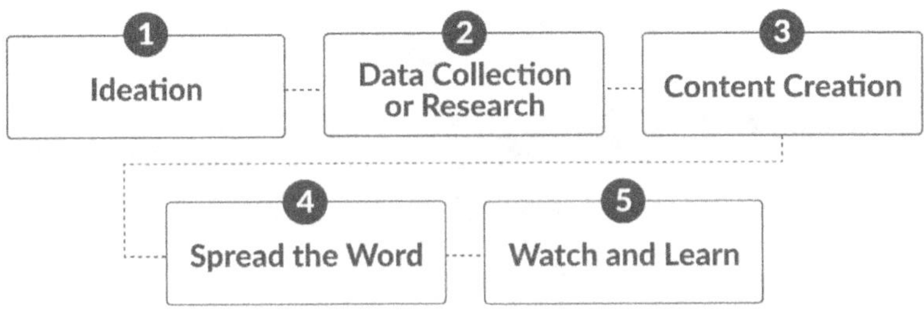

1. Ideation

Before you can run any campaign, not just in digital PR, you need an idea. What will it be about? If you want people to talk about it – and link to it – there are a few things to keep in mind when you bounce off ideas:

- Is this a newsworthy story?
- Is it going to speak to the right audience and media? (Identify first: Who is your target audience?)
- If the main angle does not work, are there other angles to pitch to journalists?
- Is it time-sensitive and, if yes, will we get it out on time?
- Is it adding additional value, or has it been done before?
- Is it in line with your brand without being advertising?

A highly time-sensitive topic, but also highly relevant for a wide audience, is this 'safecation' index.

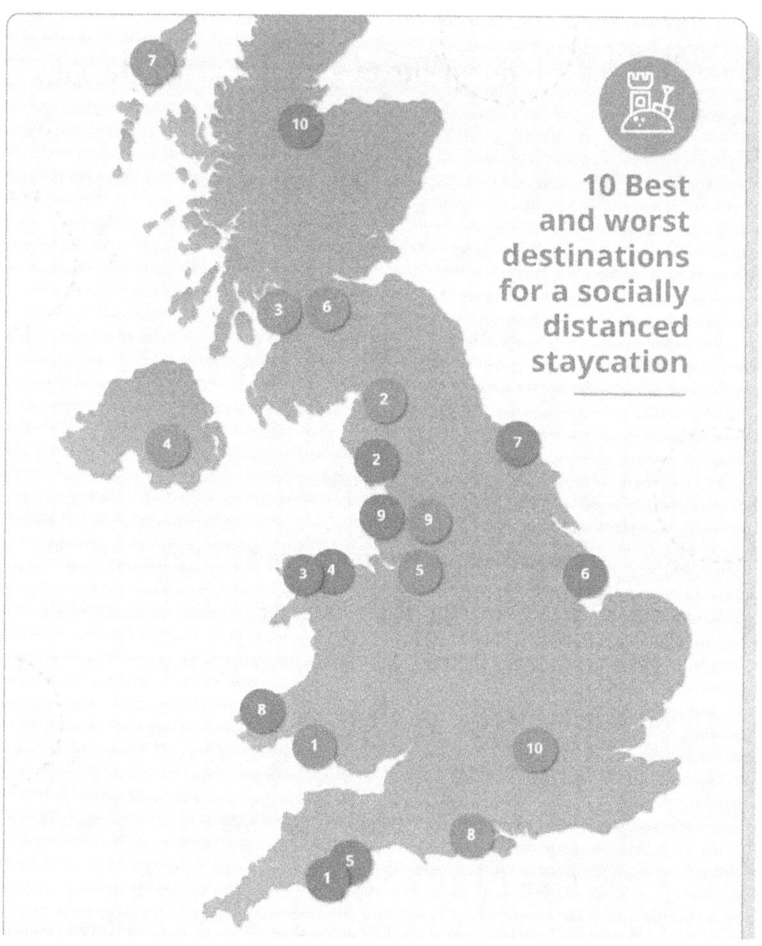

The map and a detailed list were launched in 2021, and tell you which are the best and worst destinations in the UK, for a socially distanced staycation. It is something the world had been waiting for, and therefore, gained a lot of attention.

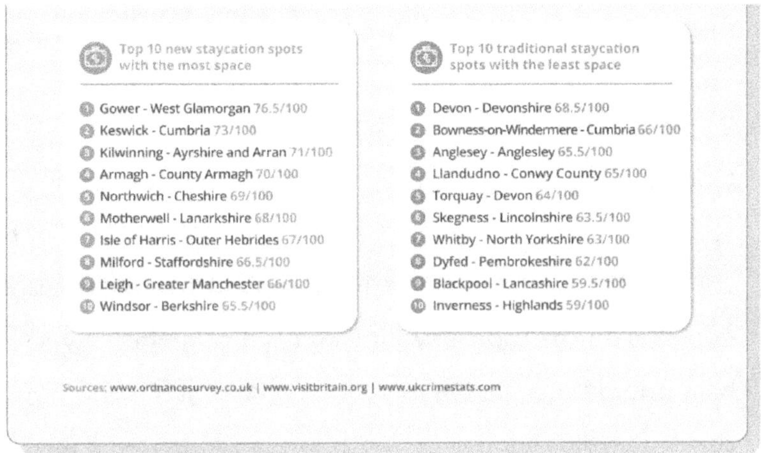

However, there are some downsides, as this campaign will only be relevant for a short period, and it will require constant updates, as the information can change at any time. The creators also took a risk, because creating such a campaign takes some time and the topic is of such relevancy, that others might have thought of it too, and could launch the day before.

A campaign about dog-friendly holidays is the perfect example of a campaign that allows multiple outreach angles. The obvious are pet-friendly and holiday-related websites that might be interested in the data and the supporting information. Adding an ordered list of UK cities, makes the campaign relevant for local press, tourism boards, or tourist attractions in those locations.

2. Data Collection or Research

Once you know what your campaign will be about, the next step is to collect the data that will become the basis of the content for your campaign. How you get this data entirely depends on the topic of your campaign. Sometimes, you will have the data available in your business intelligence, other times it will require in-depth research or even market research surveys. How complex this process might be, should not be a reason for you to not pursue a specific topic for your campaign, but you should be honest about the work it requires.

3. Content Creation

Now that you have your data ready, what are you going to do with it? When you were discussing the idea in the first step, you might have had something in mind. When looking at the data, is that still suitable? Does the type of content you are going to create resonate with your audience and with the journalists you want to reach out to?

There are plenty of content types, and some of them are more suitable for each situation than others:

If Your Data Is Number Heavy:	You might want to visualise it in an infographic that summarises your main findings.
If Your Data Has Scientific Character:	If that would resonate with your audience, you might want to think about a white paper.
If Your Topic Is Complex:	If explaining your data requires detailed information and imagery, maybe a video is a good idea.
Other Types of Content You Could Create:	Podcasts, videos, images, memes, infographics (static and interactive), virtual reality content, quizzes, blog posts, personality tests, interviews, eBooks, and webinars.

It mostly depends on the data you have and who you are trying to reach, but you should keep in mind that some of these content assets require a lot of work. For an infographic (you most likely need a designer), for a video (you might need a videographer), for a white paper (you would want an academic writer or at the very least a proofreader), and virtual reality or interactive pieces (might even require programming skills).

You might want to try some free tools to create it yourself, but you want quality above all else. Publishing a poorly made campaign can damage your brand, and it will not get you the attention you want.

4. Spread the Word

Now that you have amazing content published on your website, you need to tell the world about it – and not just anybody. You want to reach journalists, bloggers, and webmasters who could pick it up, reference your content, and link back to your website. How do you find those contacts? And more importantly, how do you get their contact details?

Many PRs are building their relationships on *X* (formerly known as *Twitter*), but that takes time, and it does not mean that there will be a suitable contact for any type of campaign in an existing network. You might have the contact of the politics editor at a national newspaper, but that will not get you far if your content is about sports. Alternatively, you can research the internet for websites that have published similar content — however, finding the contact details is a different story. There are tools such as *Roxhill, Gorkana* or *Cision* that have extensive databases for any topic, but these tools require a certain budget.

Apart from that, you mostly need to budget for time, because outreach is a full-time job and journalists will not wait three days for you to reply to their follow-up questions. Keep that in mind when you start outreaching.

5. Watch and Learn

If you got all the previous steps right, you probably have some really strong backlinks now pointing to your campaign, your rankings have increased, and your website is getting more traffic, or not? Would you even have data ready to support these statements? If not, it is time to get it, because it is hard to speak of a successful campaign, if you are not monitoring the results.

Instead of just looking at the number of links you received, you should also look at the websites that these links are coming from. Are those the websites you wanted to get attention from? Are they authoritative and trustworthy? Do they mention your brand in the right way? Do they drive any traffic? You also want to look at the impact it had on your website rankings and traffic. If there was no significant movement in any of these areas, look at your overall campaign again and at the responses you received. You might find ways to improve it or learn a thing or two for your next campaign.

3.3 Domain Authority vs Domain Rating

Written by: Lauren Henley

We've all been there: obsessing over domain authority, domain rating, and a whole host of metrics, only to wonder if there's more to the story. Spoiler alert — there is. The best type of links? Well, they're a bit like that secret sauce — you can't just slap a single metric on them and call it a day. In the digital world, these metrics are not just about numbers; they need context and considerations to get real insights. Understanding digital metrics, like domain authority and domain rating, can get pretty tricky. It's important to know that figuring out good links involves more than just looking at one number.

While metrics are useful for comparing things, the real power comes when you look at a bunch of them together. It's a bit like putting puzzle pieces together to see the entire picture. But, before you become a pro at using these metrics, it's crucial to know that not all metrics are the same. Understanding the differences is like solving a mystery and finding the right metric for your digital goals.

So, get ready to dig in and understand the world of digital PR metrics...

What is Domain Authority?

Moz domain authority (DA) is a numerical representation of a website's overall authority in search engine rankings, scored on a scale from 0 to 100. The score is influenced primarily by the quality and quantity of external backlinks pointing to the site, with additional considerations for factors like the diversity of link sources and *MozRank*. A higher DA generally suggests a stronger likelihood of favourable search engine rankings. However, it's important to note that while DA can provide a quick snapshot of a site's authority, it may not account for other crucial SEO elements, and overreliance on it may lead to overlooking specific page-level strengths or weaknesses. Additionally, frequent changes to *Moz's* algorithms may impact the consistency of DA scores over time.

What is Domain Rating?

Ahrefs domain rating (DR) is a metric designed to assess the overall authority of a website on a scale from 0 to 100. The score is influenced primarily by the quantity and quality of backlinks pointing to the entire domain. Factors such as the diversity of link sources and the overall strength of these links contribute to the DR. A higher DR typically indicates a stronger and more authoritative website. However, it's important to note that while DR provides a useful overview, it doesn't consider other essential SEO factors, and its accuracy may vary depending on the specific characteristics of the backlink profile. Users should complement DR with other metrics for a more comprehensive evaluation of a website's SEO performance. Just like with *Moz* domain authority, *Ahrefs* domain rating is a snapshot of a website's authority in the online world. It's not the only measure, but when you see a high DR, you can generally bet that the website is in the popular crowd of the internet!

DA and DR — Similarities and Differences

	Domain Authority	Domain Rating
Who Makes It?	Moz	Ahrefs
Volume of Backlinks	✓	✓
Predicts Ranking Ability	✓	✓
Quality of Backlinks	✓	✓
Outgoing Links From Referring Domains	✓	✓
Includes No-Follow Links	✗	✗
Ranking Factor Used by *Google*	✗	✗

Moz Domain Authority (DA)

- **Analogy:** Picture domain authority (DA) as the pinnacle of a skyscraper in a bustling city. On a scale from 0 to 100, it serves as a measure of a website's comprehensive strength. A higher score corresponds to an elevated level of authority in the digital landscape.
- **Factors at Play:** *Moz* looks at factors like the number and quality of backlinks to a site. It's like judging a knight by the quality of their allies and how many battles they've won.
- **Focus on Trustworthiness:** It's about having good, reliable connections rather than sheer quantity.

Ahrefs Domain Rating (DR)

- **Coolness Factor:** Picture DR as the coolness factor at a party. It's a score from 0 to 100, where a higher score means the website is cooler, or more authoritative.
- **Friendship Circle:** *Ahrefs* looks at the number and quality of referring domains (websites that link to it). It's like saying, "The more popular parties you're invited to, the cooler you are".
- **Diversity Matters:** DR considers the diversity of your backlink portfolio. It's not just about having powerful friends; it's about having a mix of friends from different circles.

In a nutshell, both are trying to measure a website's authority, but they use slightly different criteria. Ultimately, using both can give you a more comprehensive view of a website's online prowess.

How to Use DA and DR in the Right Way

In the realm of digital strategy, it's not uncommon to see domain authority or domain rating being misapplied. The key to harnessing the true power of these metrics lies in a comparative approach. When evaluating domains for link-building endeavours, it's most effective to assess domain authority or domain rating within a curated list of target publications.

Similarly, for your own domain, adopting a benchmarking strategy over time against competitors proves invaluable. This practice unveils insights into which competitors are securing a higher volume of quality links, and providing a significant edge in the nuanced landscape of competitive analysis.

More Metrics That Matter

- **Ahrefs URL Rating:** Ahrefs URL Rating is a score from 0 to 100 that measures the strength of a specific page's backlink profile — indicating how influential and authoritative that particular page is.

- **Moz Page Authority:** This is a metric on a scale of 0 to 100, estimating the likelihood of a specific page to rank well in search engine results, based on its link profile and other factors.

- **Majestic Trust Flow:** A metric that gauges the quality of a webpage's backlinks, emphasising trustworthy and reputable links, and is scored on a scale from 0 to 100.

- **Share of Search:** This metric that estimates the portion of total online search queries within a specific industry or market that a brand or website is capturing. This reflects its visibility and competitiveness in search engine results.

3.4 Relevance and What Constitutes It

Written by: Lauren Henley

In the dynamic world of digital PR, where every link is a piece of a complex puzzle, relying solely on metrics to gauge their impact might miss the subtle nuances. We acknowledge that in the realm of link building and digital PR, relevance takes centre stage. Yet, measuring relevance is no straightforward task — at times, it teeters on the edge of subjectivity. The significance of a backlink and its coverage varies from one domain to another, posing a compelling question: What truly constitutes relevance in this intricate landscape?

Join us as we delve into the depths of this chapter, unravelling the layers to understand the elusive concept of relevance in the context of link building:

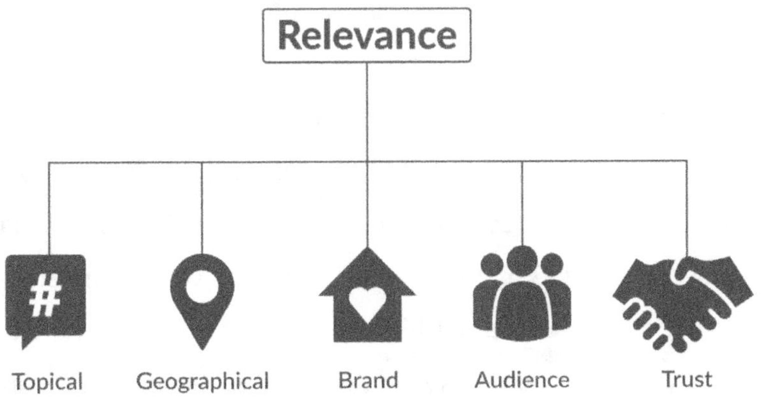

Topical Relevance

In the intricate world of digital presence, topical relevance emerges as a pivotal consideration. Ensuring that your content aligns with the current discourse in your industry is paramount. A key aspect of this relevance lies in securing coverage from authoritative publications within your niche. When these publications, recognised as authorities in relevant fields, link back to your domain, they not only endorse your content but also pass on their established authority, bolstering your domain's credibility.

Beyond the immediate impact on authority, the benefits ripple through to reaching the right audience. By securing coverage in publications that resonate with your expertise, your article gains exposure to the audience most likely to engage with your brand. This not only aids in brand awareness but also contributes to the strategic positioning of your content within the relevant discourse.

Moreover, the significance of topical relevance extends beyond mere exposure. For on-site content, links play a pivotal role in supporting and strengthening the contextual relevance of your material. When your website is linked by authoritative sources within your field, it not only enhances your credibility but also contributes to *Google's* nuanced understanding of your website. In essence, building links and coverage within the realms of your expertise becomes a strategic move in fortifying your brand's standing in the digital landscape.

Geographical Relevance

In the ever-evolving landscape of digital strategy, the era of indiscriminate link building across global territories has rightfully faded into obscurity. Today, the emphasis lies not just on amassing links, but on strategically aligning them with the brand's mission and service areas.

If your link-building strategy extends to regions beyond your operational reach, it's worth reconsidering the priorities. Rather than prioritising sheer link quantity, the focus should shift towards building a brand presence in regions where services are offered. This nuanced approach involves specifically targeting domains that share the same top-level domain or possess an audience within the countries where your services are available.

In essence, the modern link-building strategy is not merely about quantity but about precision and strategic alignment. By cultivating links and coverage in territories relevant to your operational footprint, the emphasis shifts from indiscriminate link acquisition to building brand awareness in the right places.

Brand Relevance

In digital PR, the most valuable links are the ones embedded within publications where your brand aspires to make a mark. Across every industry, there exists a selection of dream publications – those prestigious platforms whose endorsement signifies a significant vote of confidence.

However, it's crucial to recognise that the publication alone doesn't solely determine brand relevance. Beyond the choice of platform, the narrative itself plays a pivotal role. Questions arise: Are your key stakeholders featured prominently? Does the article convey your core selling messages, while portraying your brand positively? These considerations become essential checkpoints in evaluating the brand relevance of a piece of coverage. Digital PR, in essence, transcends the mere exercise of building links. When executed with precision, it evolves into a powerful tool for brand growth. Beyond the strategic placement of links, the art of digital PR lies in crafting narratives that not only secure valuable placements, but also contribute to the organic growth and positive perception of your brand.

Audience Relevance

In the digital landscape, the impact of being featured in an article is contingent on whether an audience is there to witness it. Simply gaining coverage in a publication that doesn't resonate with your target audience may secure a backlink, but does little to bolster your brand.

Digital PR practitioners must possess a keen understanding of the demographics and target customers associated with the brands they work on. This knowledge serves as a compass, guiding the selection of the most relevant publications to pitch to. By tailoring content to align with the preferences and interests of the target audience, a more engaged readership is cultivated.

This strategic alignment not only enhances reader engagement, but also reinforces the authority of the pages where your links are housed. In essence, the effectiveness of digital PR lies not just in securing coverage, but in ensuring that the right audience is there to receive and engage with it.

Trust

In an era marked by heightened media scepticism, and with *Google's* E-E-A-T guidelines underscoring the importance of trust, embedding trustworthiness into your digital PR strategy is paramount. Trust, in this context, operates on a dual axis — the reader's trust in the publication and *Google's* trust in its credibility as a reputable website.

Institutions like *Reuters* contribute to this landscape by conducting research into the most trustworthy journalists and publications, gauging public opinion. Additionally, tracking the social sentiment surrounding news outlets offers valuable insights into how much readers value the information shared.

While metrics such as DA and DR offer a glimpse into a website's trustworthiness, it's crucial to acknowledge that these are not absolute measures. They provide a part of the picture, considering various factors that contribute to a site's overall trust. In navigating the intricate realm of digital PR, understanding and enhancing both aspects of trust is pivotal for fostering credibility and authority.

Ways to Measure Relevance

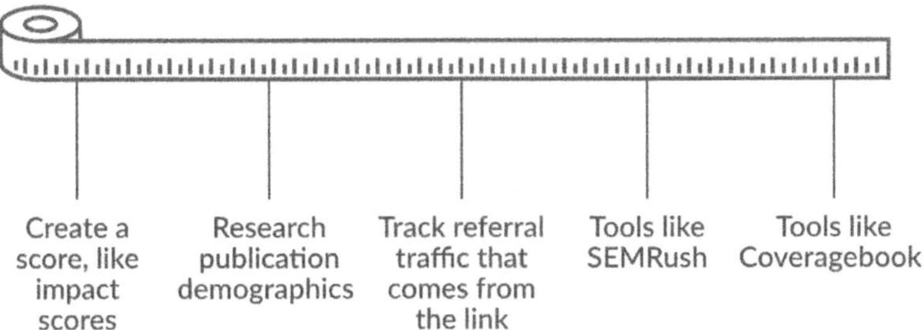

Chapter 4: Google Search Algorithms and Their Impact

4.1 Overview

Written by: Andrew Holland

Google didn't invent the internet. It wasn't even the first search engine. That title goes to something called *Archie*. But *Google* made the internet easier to access. It gave us better results and faster, too. Even today, where *Google* has around an 89% market share, other search engines aren't anywhere near as good as *Google*. But what makes it so good? The answer is its algorithms.

What Google Algorithms Are and Why They Exist

Google's algorithms are complex systems used to retrieve data from its vast search index and instantly deliver the best possible search results for a query. These algorithms are a blend of automated processes and mathematical formulas that analyse hundreds of variables, or 'signals'. They then rank web pages in order of relevance and quality for any given search term.

Purpose of Google Algorithms

The primary purpose of *Google's* algorithms is to provide users with the most relevant, high-quality search results, as quickly as possible. As the internet has grown exponentially, these algorithms have become essential in filtering through the endless sea of information, to present users with content that is both useful and trustworthy. Without these algorithms, finding valuable information amidst the vast amount of content on the web would be an overwhelming task. After all, the goal of great SEO is to align a website with *Google* and leverage best practices to aid in the site's discovery. So, just how do the algorithm updates alter SEO?

The Impact of Google Algorithm Updates on SEO

The relationship between *Google's* algorithm updates and search engine optimisation is continuous evolution. Each major update has reshaped the SEO landscape, often requiring web admins and SEO professionals to adapt strategies, to maintain or improve their search engine rankings.

The impact of these updates can be seen in several key areas:

Content Quality and Relevance

Updates have underscored the importance of high-quality, relevant content. Websites with thin, duplicate, or low-value content saw their rankings plummet, while those offering valuable, in-depth information on user queries, rose to prominence. This shift has made content quality a cornerstone of effective SEO strategies.

Link Building Practices

Google took action and created a range of updates to reduce practices such as buying links, excessive link exchanges, or using irrelevant and low-quality links for SEO. In the past, SEOs took to search engines and manipulated *Google* by gaining links at scale. This altered the quality of the search engine results, and *Google's* ongoing updates have changed how most SEOs build links.

Mobile Optimisation

With the advent of *Mobilegeddon*, *Google* made it clear that mobile-friendliness is a critical ranking factor. In fact, *Google* is now a mobile-first index. Websites that aren't optimised for mobile devices not only provide a poor user experience, but also suffer in search rankings. This update pushed SEOs and website owners to adopt responsive design and consider mobile users' needs in their SEO strategies.

User Experience (UX)

Google's algorithm updates increasingly prioritise the user experience. Factors like site speed, easy navigation, and user journey have become integral to SEO. Enhancements in these areas can lead to better engagement, lower bounce rates, and ultimately, higher rankings.

OK, so we can see how updates impact search, and we know that *Google* always wants to bring the best results to users. But why do they keep needing to make updates?

The Dark Side of the SEO Industry

Google constantly updates its search engine to ensure it remains the best. However, there is just one problem: the SEO industry. The SEO industry has a few sides to it. On the one hand, we have search engine optimisation that adheres to *Google's* best practices. On the other hand, we have an SEO industry that will do whatever it takes to rank a website and generate traffic. We lovingly call these sides of the industry 'white' and 'black hat' SEO.

Generally speaking, the difference between white hat and black hat SEO is quite simple. White hat SEO seeks to optimise a website for discovery online, black hat SEO seeks to manipulate *Google's* rankings to benefit themselves.

But why is this a problem?

The Problem With Black Hat SEO

If *Google* aims to bring the best results to their search engine users, but people can manipulate the results — this means that the best results aren't being shown. And if the best results aren't being shown, their users will leave to find other search engines. For this reason, *Google* continually updates its algorithms to ensure the best results are returned for users. This is where we often see websites go from ranking highly to nearly disappearing from search. And I've seen brands making thousands of pounds daily to have their traffic vanish overnight.

Black hat SEO can provide fast results, but as it's a manipulation and not an attempt to provide the best results for search users, very often, *Google* will provide an update that limits these black hat techniques.

4.2 Key Updates Over the Last Few Years

Written by: Andrew Holland

If you've been involved in SEO for a while, two updates send shivers down the spines of SEOs. These are known as *Panda* and *Penguin*. *Panda* hit around 2011 and targeted low-quality websites that were ranking online. *Penguin* came later and was focused on backlink profiles. These two updates destroyed websites and laid the foundation for today's *Google* results.

Since the days of *Panda* and *Penguin*, many updates have followed, and with each update, *Google* targets a way to improve its search results. And this impacts a lot of websites. However, over the last few years, *Google* has rolled out updates that people are still struggling to overcome.

But what are these updates actually targeting?

Updates Are Designed to Make Things Better... But They Don't Always

As this is written, we're in the middle of a sea of updates from *Google*. And the results are not great, so why are they doing this? Among the many reasons is that, again, SEOs have been up to naughty stuff. If it's not flooding the internet with thousands of AI-generated pages of content, it's creating content that doesn't really add any new information or value. And if you sprinkle in the fact that there are concerns over the younger generations relying on *TikTok* for information — you can see what a problem this is becoming.

So, *Google* has created a range of updates that have tried to deal with the issues. However, this has also resulted in new issues. By the time you read this, those issues might have been resolved, they might not, and new updates may have come along. But if we have a look at the recent ones that have caused devastation, it will reveal learning points we can use in the future.

December 2022 Link Spam Update

The *link spam* update was exactly as you might expect, an update that targets link manipulation. But what was different, is that this update was the first to use the machine-learning, spam prevention system, known as *Spambrain*. While *SpamBrain* might be an odd name, it certainly is effective. In fact, it is so effective that it has destroyed websites caught out buying links.

Here's what *Google* has to say about their 2022 update and *SpamBrain*:

Our launch today, which we refer to as the December 2022 **link spam update***, will take about two weeks to fully roll out.*

Ranking may change as spammy links are neutralized and any credit passed by these unnatural links are lost. This launch will affect all languages.

As we have always emphasized, links obtained primarily for artificial manipulation of search rankings are link spam. Our algorithms and manual actions aim to nullify these unnatural links at scale, and we will continue to improve our coverage.

— **Google** on their 2022
update and *SpamBrain*

The critical thing to remember is that *SpamBrain* is always on. It actively looks for sites that use links to artificially manipulate rankings. So, if you've engaged in any kind of link buying, *SpamBrain* might come for you when you least want it or expect it.

March and August 2023 Core Update

These updates were generally focused on sites that were not displaying E-E-A-T (experience, expertise, authority, and trustworthiness). However, while E-E-A-T is not a ranking factor, *Google* is looking for signals on your site that trigger ranking factors that are aligned with E-E-A-T. I appreciate that this sometimes feels like we're talking in a different language with E–E-A-T, *SpamBrain*, updates, and signals — but these are the terms that *Google* uses, and keeping up with them is useful. But again, *Google* is trying to find genuine sites with these updates, and reward people who are not great at SEO, but good at what they do.

September 2023 Helpful Content Update

If the core updates didn't rock you enough, the helpful content update probably finished many off. In *Google's* own words:

*The **helpful content system** aims to reward better content where visitors feel they've had a satisfying experience, while content that doesn't meet a visitor's expectations won't perform as well.*

— **Google** on their *helpful content system*

This is where many SEOs and websites really put their heads into their hands. For so long, content was just a curation and repetition of what was already ranking, articles were combined and rewritten to make them longer and bigger. And that is how the last few years of content for organic search has been created. The helpful content update changed everything and saw websites nose-dive in traffic gains. To put it lightly, it's been a bumpy ride for organic search and SEO for a while. The key learning point is that each and every update is all about getting the best results to the user — and that should be the priority of every SEO.

March 2024 Core Update

Google's March 2024 Core Update was a big one. To give you the lowdown, fast, it's focused on three areas:

1. Expired Domain Abuse: Where websites are purchased and repurposed to manipulate search.
2. Scaled Content Abuse: This involves mass-generating low-value AI content.
3. Site Reputation Abuse: Where third-party pages are published with the view to manipulate search rankings.

This wasn't like other updates. *Google* has made numerous changes, and sites are being de-indexed from search rankings. *Google* has been using an AI tool called *SpamBrain* to detect link networks for some time now.

This update is targeted at something called 'parasite SEO', a term coined by black hat SEOs, to create content on third-party sites and add links to their websites/affiliate products. An example would be creating a super thin article on *Medium* or *LinkedIn* and ramming it with affiliate links. It could rank based on the sheer power of the domain authority, but it shouldn't.

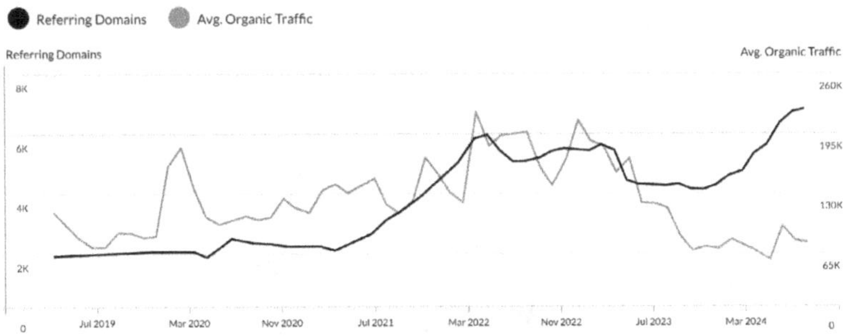

This was a muscle upgrade to their already existing *Spambrain* AI. However, in that same spam policy, they also target the creation of low-value content for links. All these updates are warning signals from *Google* to SEOs to clean up their act and stop trying to spam the web. *Google* is actively hunting for *link spam*, and it's getting better at it. But one thing is clear — *Google* wants to reward sites and brands that have and openly display E-E-A-T — and the next step is to figure that out.

4.3 E.E.A.T

Written by: Andrew Holland

We've used the word E-E-A-T a few times now, and if you're reading this, there's a good chance you know what it is. But I hope to give you a new way of looking at E-E-A-T. As we've said previously, E-E-A-T stands for experience, expertise, authority, and trustworthiness. It was originally just E-A-T, as they didn't have the word 'experience' in, and added that in December 2022.

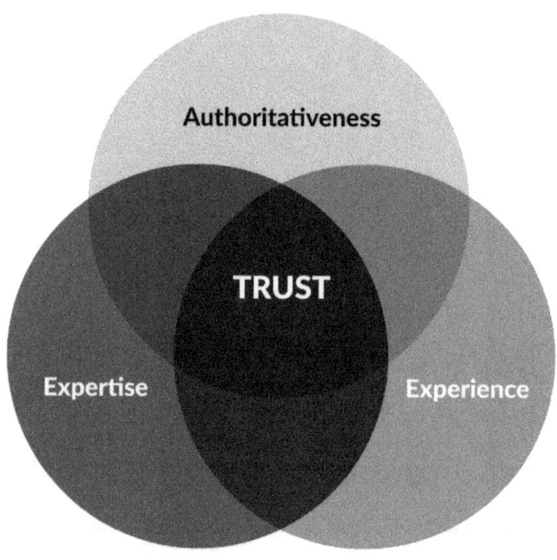

When I say add, I mean they included this in their search rater guidelines. The search rater guidelines are used by

Google's team of search raters, who evaluate the performance of their search ranking systems. It's better to think of them as the judges on *X-Factor*. They manually look at your site and assess if it would satisfy the search engine user who typed in the query. It's their feedback that helps *Google* to shape their algorithms.

I'll spare you the need to read the full 166-page document, instead, I'll sum up what E-E-A-T is in one word… brand. The term 'brand' can be given a wide range of definitions, but I like to call it the sum total of your marketing. And it's what people think of when they think of you or discover your business. Search raters assess your site and feed this data back to *Google*, which then uses this to develop their search engines further. But all E-E-A-T is really providing *Google* with, is enough information to know who you are, why you're an expert, and why people should trust you.

I have a simple formula to help you determine if your brand displays the E-E-A-T signals that *Google* loves:

Evidence from the Past and Evidence for the Present = E-E-A-T.

The evidence from the past is everything you've done so far for your brand or business to be classed as 'authoritative'.

Now, I have a neat method to help you try to understand your evidence of the past, envision yourself as an expert witness who has been hired to give evidence in court. In this scenario, *Google* operates as the judge, and you must articulate your expertise and qualifications to both the judge and the jury, to explain why they should listen to you. Being recognised as an expert witness entails a rigorous vetting process. You should consider this the same for your website.

E-E-A-T demands that you establish and verify your authority and proficiency in your specific area of expertise — and here are a few ways to prove your E-E-A-T:

	Ways to Prove Your E-E-A-T	
Educational background and qualifications		Recognitions and awards received
Implemented policies	Client testimonials	Professional journey
Relevant case studies	Scholarly articles and publications	Mentions in the media
Geographical location	Ways to contact you	Social proof

Look at your website and brand and ask yourself if they have any/much of the above, contained within your site or the sites of others. For example, you might have a lot of positive reviews on *Trustpilot* that are housed on their site, which you reference on yours, too. Or perhaps you've been featured in the media, and you display this on your site with an 'as featured in' section or even a media page. This is evidence from the past. This brings us nicely to evidence for the present.

Evidence for the present is your marketing to show the world you're an expert. This list includes:

Creative advertising	**Evidence for the Present**	Helpful content for search
Helpful content, not for search	New insights and data creation	Publicity
Book writing	Guest posts (on real sites with real traffic)	Developing your authorship profiles
Podcast production	Podcast appearances	Links
Media mentions	Social media content	Social media perspectives (others talking about you)

Budget dictates what you can do, but budget typically revolves a lot around time, and that's the thing with E-E-A-T. It's not really about ROI, it's about brand marketing. You are displaying your brand to as many people as possible, and this will naturally fall into the search engines as they crawl digital assets. If you're reading the above and thinking, 'That's everyone's job', you're right. E-E-A-T is something that every marketing department is involved in, regardless of whether they are aware of this or not. However, this is also the power of digital PR, because digital PR actually ticks off a lot on that list. The effectiveness of digital PR for SEO cannot be underestimated, but equally, digital PR does more for brands than just help to increase rankings. And it's this that makes digital PR, not something for brands to consider, but something that all brands need to have.

Auditing Your E-E-A-T

One of the best ways to audit your E–E-A-T is to ask someone else. You are way too close to your own site to be able to give a decent assessment. Search professionals who understand E-E-A-T will be able to give a thorough assessment.

I have three methods that you can use to gain an overview:

1. The Brand Search Test

This is a simple test and takes seconds, just head to *Google* and search for your brand name. What comes up? Do you have a knowledge panel, or is it your website followed by your social media handles? Perhaps it's not even you? You can't control what comes up in brand search, but you can create more opportunities to come up with positive brand signals. You want to ensure that good things about your brand and doorways into learning more about you show up. But how? Digital PR will help with this, but you can also achieve this through good-quality social media assets. Appearing on podcasts is another good way to increase the likelihood that great content about your brand shows up.

2. The News Test

This is another easy test to conduct. Search for your brand in *Google* and then hit the news tab. Do you show up? If not, keep scrolling. Still nothing? Well, if that's the case, it should serve as a warning that you need to do something newsworthy.

3. The Instant Reaction

This is my favourite test: find five websites in various sectors and ask someone (ideally a stranger) to look at all five. You only want them to look for 30 seconds at each website, and then ask them to evaluate each. Just ask for their opinions on the site, if they would trust the business, what they do, and what they think of the site and the business. If you can't find someone you don't know to do it, this is one of those things that parents are good for.

Of course, you want one of the five websites to be your brand, but you will gain valuable information from that first impression. Make this as fast and as furious as you can. We don't want people to make logical breakdowns — this is just about feelings, and, of course, this isn't scientific. However, you'd be surprised at the odd things people say, and this can provide you with information that you wouldn't have considered.

If you run the first three tests, you'll have a good idea if your brand is doing an excellent job around E-E-A-T. However, you also have to understand that E-E-A-T is something that comes from deliberate marketing. Experts display expertise, experts get cited, experts provide expert commentary, and experts also provide data and analysis on their industry. And this is why digital PR is the fuel for better E-E-A-T.

Chapter 5: The Digital PR Process

5.1 Ideation

Written by: James Renhard

Nurturing the Power of Creativity in Digital PR Campaigns

Digital media never stays still. It's constantly evolving, and being pushed or pulling in various directions, so your digital PR campaigns have to reflect that. As such, at the heart of every successful PR campaign lies the ability to generate innovative, topical, and intelligent ideas. Ideation — the process of conceiving and conceptualising concepts and strategies — is the foundation for impactful digital PR campaigns. Drawing on decades of experience in digital media that's seen the creation of many good campaigns, some award-winning ones, and my fair share of stinkers. This article will explore the essence of ideation, breaking down the steps required to foster a culture of creativity that you can apply to your digital PR approach.

Understanding Ideation

Before diving head-first into the ball pool of creative ideation, it's crucial to understand the core principles of ideation. Would life be much easier for all of us in marketing, if we could just flick a switch and come up with original, thought-provoking, creative ideas? Yes. But, until that day comes, generating creative ideas needs to start with generating an environment, where ideas are not just welcome, but they can thrive, and be built into powerful campaigns.

Establishing a Creative Culture

Creativity flourishes in collaborative environments, where diverse perspectives, opinions, interests, and approaches can melt together. Fostering an environment that encourages open communication and collaboration is like rocket fuel for successful ideation. Even if you're doing this alone, be open to other ideas, thoughts, philosophies, and perspectives.

I do hold a sneaking suspicion he wasn't talking specifically about digital PR, but in a quote painted on many a pub wall, Anthony Bourdain once said:

Go somewhere you've never been. Listen to someone you think may have nothing in common with you ... Be open to a world where you may not understand or agree with the person next to you, but have a drink with them anyways.

— **Anthony Bourdain**

It's a maxim that's at the very heart of creativity; be open to diverse thinking. Furthermore, a key element in encouraging a creative space is safety. Embracing failure, and knowing that it's a virtual certainty, is a must. People have to feel safe to get it wrong, long before they get it right.

Again, dipping into my Big Book of Quotes Taken From Inspirational Posters, Ernest Hemingway is credited as telling us...

"The thing is to become a master and, in your old age, to acquire the courage to do what children did when they knew nothing."

— *Ernest Hemingway*

Hemingway knew that taking risks, putting ideas out there into the world, and sometimes getting it wrong, is central to successful creativity. You should feel comfortable taking risks and viewing failures as opportunities to learn and iterate.

Research and Insights

It's a common misconception to believe that creativity is a boundary-free, free fall through the wilds of your imagination. That's not creativity. That's Friday night at Glastonbury, right before you start cuddling your wellies. No, creativity needs a framework, it needs boundaries and understanding set by research and insights.

Successful ideation begins with a deep, intentional, researched understanding of whom you're creating content for. You need to know the brand you're speaking on behalf of, who they are, what's important to them, and what makes sense for them to speak about. You need to know who you're trying to reach — your intended audience. And you need to know the people you're going to pitch your content to — who's going to be so impressed with what you've done, they want a piece of it on their own domain.

You should also look at the brand competitors, and identify white spaces and opportunities in the industry. Is there a gap? Can you add more? Can you lead the conversation, or even change it?

Workshopping Ideas

Many creative people are different and discover a way of working that best suits them. However, the consensus among many, and my preferred way of working — assuming the above steps are in place — is to start my creative thinking alone, before bringing my ideas to other people for peer and stakeholder feedback.

I like to start by exploring the topics, themes, trends, and narratives around the sector I want to create a campaign for. I like to pull different ideas together, work up thoughts, let my ideas drift, build on them, and take them back a step, or two steps. It can be the fun part of ideation, but it can be positively tortuous when things don't seem to click. But time, exploration, and finding a new angle or view of the ideas you're working on more often than not, can conjure the kernel of an idea, seemingly out of nowhere.

The next stage, if you have the luxury of not doing this alone, is workshopping your ideas. Often called brainstorming, this is where you and a group of people — remember that diverse group from earlier? This is them — you and a group of people work up the ideas you and, ideally they, have brought to the session following solo ideation. Utilise various workshopping techniques, such as mind mapping and deconstructing ideas, to stretch and test the concepts that you have. Be brave, be open, and don't be afraid to let your ideas try to fly, even if they end up falling flat on the ground. Refine and reshape your ideas, tear them apart and build them back up. This, after all, is what the workshop is for.

Conclusion

In digital PR, creative ideation propels campaigns to new heights. By cultivating a culture of collaboration, embracing failure as a learning opportunity, conducting thorough research, and refining ideas, you can unlock the full potential of ideation. The art of ideation goes beyond generating ideas — it's about fostering an environment where innovation thrives, shaping the success of digital PR campaigns.

5.2 Testing and Refining

Written by: James Renhard

Why Testing and Refinement Should Be at the Heart of Your Digital PR Practice

As has previously been established, the landscape of digital media is constantly evolving and changing. A strategy that's worked well in the past won't necessarily guarantee you success forever. The solution, happily, is a fairly straightforward, if often overlooked one — testing and refining.

Testing: The Bedrock of Digital PR

Testing in digital PR is not just a step in the process, it's the bedrock. It involves rigorously evaluating strategies, content, and campaigns to ensure they resonate with the intended audience.

In digital PR, this testing phase helps identify what connects with the audience, what falls flat, and what needs tweaking. So, what should you test? The answer is as easy as the results are rewarding, you should test everything. Every. Thing. Try different kinds of campaigns, fire out different kinds of pitches, and experiment with different headlines. Test whether putting images in pitches helps, putting them higher, lower, smaller, in a link, or as an attachment. Do you put a statistic in your subject line? Do you tease the lead, or spell your findings out? Does it all work the same for different sectors or different publications? *(Spoiler: no. No, it does not).*

Test when you pitch, test who you pitch to, and test how long your pitch emails should be, where you add a link, or how many links you add. I could go on. The message is, if it's something you're doing for digital PR, test it, and test it again. And test it tomorrow, and the day after, and the day after that. Because testing equals data, and data equals understanding. And when you understand that little bit more, that's when you can start to refine what you do.

This process is similar to what Ed Catmull, co-founder of *Pixar*, calls The *Pixar* way, stating:

"Ideas only become great when they are challenged and tested."

— Ed Catmull
co-founder of Pixar

Refinement: Turning Good into Great

Let's take a quick break from the digital PR narrative here for a second. Think about social media, you will surely have seen countless videos of people cooking recipes or making cocktails. The presenter tries their creation for the first time and instantly nods and moans their approval in a wave of cerebral ecstasy. This, my friend, is a lie. A filthy, digital lie. I know this because nothing you make for the first time ever tastes that good. That wave of delight when you taste something amazing is the product of tens, or even hundreds, of attempts at getting it wrong. Then getting it a little less wrong, and then kind of good, and one day it all works. And the big secret behind this hard-won success? Refinement.

Refinement goes hand-in-hand with testing. It's about honing your message, sharpening your strategy, and fine-tuning your approach. Taking the hard-won data you've got from testing, and applying the wins. Identifying the success, taking what works, and applying it to what you're doing. While I'm very much a believer in not sitting on a good project while trying to make it perfect, like Voltaire said, *"Perfect is the enemy of good"*. Refinement, however, is the process of turning something good into something great. In the context of digital PR, refinement means taking feedback from testing and using it to improve your campaigns, your pitches, and your ideation.

Embracing the Cycle

Testing and refinement should not be seen as one-off tasks but as an ongoing, iterative process. Each campaign offers new data, insights, and opportunities to learn and improve. In digital PR, iteration is the key to innovation. But it's not just your approach that can improve with testing and refinement — you can use the results to grow leads as well. Case studies, based on what you learn, are real-world examples that underscore the value of testing and refinement. Through this ongoing process, you're learning, and developing data-backed intuition that can put you ahead of the evolutionary curve that's inherent in the industry.

Conclusion: The Path to Digital PR Excellence

In conclusion, the significance of testing and refinement in digital PR cannot be overstated. They are not merely steps in a process, but are integral to the success of any digital PR strategy. As we navigate the complex and ever-changing digital landscape, these practices will continue to be the compass that guides us towards effective and impactful digital PR campaigns.

Chapter 6: Digital PR Tactics

6.1 Hero Campaigns

Written by: James Renhard

Let's face it, it's rare that the two worlds of digital PR and boxing collide. One is a world of prime athletes, at the peak of human conditioning. Ready to take on the most primal battle imaginable for a test that's as much a test of towering mental fortitude, as it is about lightning pace and dynamite power. The other is boxing.

But if digital PR was like boxing, then hero campaigns would doubtless be the heavyweight division. Hero campaigns are the biggest, loudest, hardest-hitting, and importantly, the most noticeable of all the strategies we use. And just like with boxing, this doesn't mean that the other approaches aren't as good. In fact, purists could make strong arguments as to why some of the more agile formats are superior — but there's a reason why everyone wants to watch the heavyweights: knock-out power.

What Is a Hero Campaign

The simple answer is, that a digital PR hero campaign is an all-singing, all-dancing, large-scale campaign that uses a range of proven digital PR strategies to earn links at scale. They're campaigns that, when done right, can disrupt a sector, capture the imagination of the public, and drive game-changing results for brands. A more complex answer, although there is a vast, almost never-ending, range of hero campaigns. Generally speaking, they are long-read campaigns, backed with data that drives the narrative, and include designs that illustrate the statistics, all of which are hosted on a domain. However, the exceptions to this rule are many and varied, including Dream Job campaigns, product-focused campaigns, visual campaigns, and more.

Hero campaigns often leverage trending topics, real-world events, emotional stories, or surprising elements to capture attention rapidly and encourage sharing among an audience — something that adds significant value to journalists. Distinguished by their scale and ambition, the aim is widespread reach and high engagement.

Producing and creating a successful hero campaign involves several key steps:

Ideation and Concept Development

This is the stage where creativity and innovation are paramount. After all, if you don't have the idea, you've got nothing to build on. We looked in more depth at ideation, and the creative process, all of which should be applied to this first step in creating a hero campaign.

Originality

While there are never any guaranteed successes, there are two ways to give your hero campaign the best possible chance of success: be the first, or be the best. You can either be the first voice, speaking about a subject, breaking new ground, and genuinely leading a conversation. Or, be the best, most complete, most authoritative voice. And doing the latter usually involves some elements of saying something new anyway. So, be original.

Research and Data

Nothing kills a hero campaign faster than having holes in your research and data. It's key to take the time to thoroughly research any data, analysis, and information you're using for your hero campaign. Actively look for opposing data or opinions, test to see if your data is robust enough, and try to pick holes in it yourself.

Similarly, work on a solid methodology for your data, again, testing it for weakness, and rebuilding where you need to. It may seem counter-intuitive, but you're much better off discovering issues and fixing them at this stage, than a journalist finding them and running a piece on your wonky data in a national publication.

Attention-Grabbing Design

You want the hero campaign to grab a reader's attention immediately, and the most direct way of doing this is with design assets. The design should professionally reflect the brand, although it should not be over-branded if you want journalists to use your images. It should also always, always, be attractive enough to capture attention.

If you've got the resources to have your design assets produced by an experienced designer, it's generally worth the investment. However, tools like Canva or AI image generator Dall-E 2 can be helpful for those with budget constraints.

Captivating Copy

While the designs can draw people in, it's the copy that keeps them there, and really delivers the heart of the campaign. The content must be relevant to both the brand and its audience, aligning with the business's objectives and the audience's interests and needs. If you can weave in some natural-looking keywords, references to key verticals, find a place for some links to other pages on the domain, and scatter in some E-E-A-T signals (see chapter four for more on that), then you're on to a winner.

However, the key box that you need to tick is that your copy tells a story. What are you saying? Why are you saying it? What's the impact of your findings? How does this fit into the reader's life?

Evolving Outreach

Throughout the creation of your campaign, from the first ideation to the final sign-off, consider how you can tell the story. What angles have you got? What elements are newsworthy now? What's coming up in the news that you can hook your hero on to? Can you split your data up geographically, by interest groups, or different demographics? Is there a natural end date to your campaign, or can it be evergreen?

Really consider how to get the most out of this engaging, appealing, heavyweight thing you've just created. And when you do, measure the effectiveness of each approach. What's working? What's not? What can you change? Can you pivot the idea?

Hero campaigns are a powerful tool in the arsenal of digital PR. They combine creativity and strategic planning with deep brand understanding. This allows campaigns to not only capture attention, disrupt a sector, and leave a lasting impact on the audience, but also drive the commercial objectives of a business, with a powerful impact on SEO performance. These campaigns require a significant investment of time, resources, and creativity, but when executed successfully, they can elevate a brand's profile and create a lasting connection with both established and new audiences.

6.2 Newsjacking

Written by: Lauren Wilden

When it comes to the daily tasks that a typical digital PR faces regularly, there is a never-ending list of important jobs to keep on top of, to ensure that clients are seeing consistent results and impact on their investment. It can often be all too easy to get caught up in the process of data collection and analysis, or design and outreach planning for campaigns. Due to this, digital PRs miss one of the golden opportunities. That is, to build instant and relevant links for their accounts, with nothing more than some well-timed, expert-led commentary and insight.

A quick *Google* search will give you the following definition of newsjacking:

"The practice of taking advantage of current events or news stories in such a way, as to promote or advertise one's product or brand."

Sounds straightforward enough, doesn't it? Simply take your pick of the biggest current headlines and trending topics on social media and find a seamless way of incorporating discussion, opinions, or advice on behalf of your client and their knowledge on the matter. If only it were that simple.

The issue with newsjacking is that every PR person with clients operating in similar sectors — regardless of whether they work on the digital or more traditional side of the industry — will be consuming the same news outlets. They will be waiting to strike as soon as a relevant opportunity arises.

This sheer amount of competition from other PRs means that to cut through the noise and generate results, your own newsjacking efforts need to be as interesting, newsworthy, and relevant as possible. Trust me, if your subject line and the opening paragraph in your outreach pitch doesn't immediately grab a journalist's attention, those links and top-tier coverage aren't coming your way.

Why Is Newsjacking So Important in Digital PR?

It can be wonderful to see sites like *The BBC*, *The Telegraph* or *Forbes* cover your newsjacking comments. As digital PRs, we strive to ensure that we gear outreach of this kind towards relevant online publications and blogs. These will be most likely to include links back to clients' websites and category pages for SEO purposes. In fact, high DA (domain authority) links for some of our biggest clients' prioritised category pages, have been thanks to newsjacking. This gives journalists an incentive to direct audiences to specific on-site content, for further information on a news story.

SEO is primarily focused on making a website rank as highly as possible in organic search rankings on *Google* and other search engines. Breaking news stories — like those we create newsjacking comments and insights around — will give certain keywords and phrases importance on *Google*. This is due to the volume of internet users already searching for them, or discussing them on social media platforms.

By making sure to include some keywords and phrases in newsjacking outreach pitches, as well as in clients' on-site content, the hope is that over time, digital PRs can give these pages the same level of importance. And, ultimately, increase search rankings among competitors vying for the same positions.

Generating Coverage and Links from Newsjacking Opportunities

One of the most challenging aspects of newsjacking, undoubtedly, centres around the issue of timing. Being able to outreach comments and insight as quickly as possible after spotting an opportunity. In a perfect world, our clients are available at any time day or night to give their insight and proof an endless stream of newsjacking pitches and comments. Sadly, due to heavy workloads, PRs can often miss out on the small window of opportunity to successfully outreach.

Each breaking news alert is unique depending on the nature of the story, how ongoing the narrative is likely to be, and how many industries it directly impacts. However, as a rule of thumb, it's wise to send out a newsjacking pitch no later than three hours after the story starts generating headlines, to secure the maximum chance of coverage.

For those wary of being able to persuade clients to sign off newsjacking comments quickly enough to have an impact, here are four ways to speed up the process:

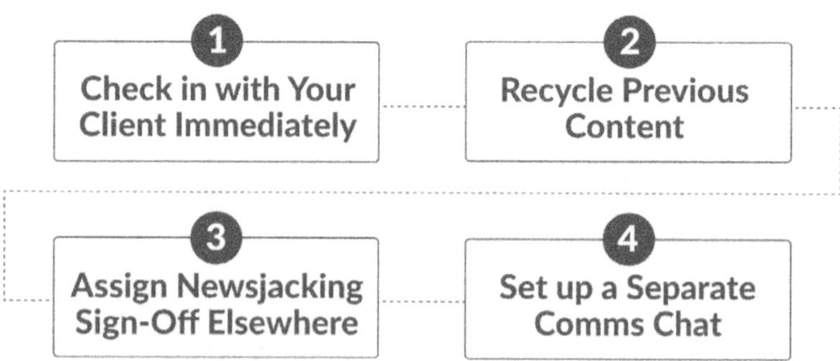

1. Check in with Your Client Immediately

It can be tempting to begin drafting up a comment on behalf of a client, as soon as you see a story break or a *Google* alert comes through. However, to avoid any wasted time, I'd always recommend running your idea past a client first. This not only gives them the heads-up that you're working on something they will need to look over ASAP, but there is always a chance the hypothetical topic is something they want to refrain from commenting on. By doing this, none of your time will be wasted drafting anything up that doesn't even get circulated.

2. Recycle Previous Content

As much as I wish I could sit here and say that every single newsjacking opportunity I've worked on during my career, has resulted in copious amounts of links and 'worldie' coverage for clients. That would, quite frankly, be a huge lie. Fortunately, I have learnt one thing from the many times a comment I've worked on has failed to deliver any coverage. That is, there is a very strong chance that the messages, tips, or advice at the centre of the insight, can be reworked at a later date for my client's benefit. It may well need some edits or additions further down the line, but the advantage of having a base to start with next time, should give you a head start in beating all the other PRs to journalists' inboxes. It's, therefore, ALWAYS worth keeping all newsjacking pitches for future reference. Similarly, if a newsjack that you work on performs particularly well, be sure to try to understand what it was about your pitch that helped it to land, and try to replicate it in your future opportunities.

3. Assign Newsjacking Sign-Off Elsewhere

When working on digital PR for a client on the smaller side, regular communication is often only with one or two individuals from the business. If these contacts hold senior or managerial positions, it can be somewhat of a struggle to get hold of them for a quick newsjacking sign-off. Being able to liaise with a more junior employee, who has the authority to 'OK' an idea and then push a comment for sign-off, is an effective way to speed up the sign-off process.

4. Set up a Separate Comms Chat

We've noticed the huge benefit of setting up dedicated *Slack* chats that are used exclusively for newsjacking purposes. These are separate from the chats where we discuss any of the wider campaigns we're concurrently working on. While certain conversations may contain messages that aren't as urgent or pressing, clients have come to realise how advantageous a fast response on the chat is for link-building efforts.

Where Should You Be Searching for Newsjacking Opportunities?

The best way to ensure you and your team are among the first to spot a breaking story that relates to your clients' industries, is by immersing yourself in the news on a global, national, and local level. The nature of the 24-hour news cycle means that the lifespan of the majority of stories will be very limited. So, waiting for the next day or Monday morning to react to a perfect opportunity is a risky move. Especially as there is a much stronger chance your pitches are likely to be read by journalists, news desks, and weekend editors during these off-peak periods.

Here are some of our tried and tested methods, that give us the best chance of being able to react as quickly as possible, when it comes to newsjacking opportunities:

- ***BBC News:*** The holy grail as far as breaking news you can trust is concerned. The business live blog on the website is great to bookmark and check regularly throughout the day, for any commentary opportunities that could relate to your clients' sector.

- **24-Hour News Channels:** With so many Digital PRs continuing to work from home -either remotely or in a hybrid set-up. Having a news channel or radio station such as BBC News, Sky News, or Times Radio on in the background can help to keep you up to date with breaking stories.

- *Google* **Alerts and** *Talkwalker* **Alerts:** These alerts are not just useful for tracking existing client coverage and brand mentions. Setting up keywords or terms that relate to existing campaigns that you want to newsjack, can be a fantastic way to ensure you're one of the first to jump on an opportunity when it arises.

- **Newsletter Subscriptions:** Signing up to receive newsletters is a great tactic for spotting who is writing about what topics, when it comes to the big-ticket publications you want to land links on. There is a huge amount of sector-specific newsletters. Some of our favourites: *Metro Lifestyle | Huffington Post UK | Reuters Morning Digest | The Daily News In Brief (SheerLuxe) | Stylist | The Telegraph.*

- **#journorequest on X (formerly Twitter):** Keep on top of the hashtag #journorequest over on X. Here, you will find an array of UK and international journalists seeking specific comments, experts, or data that you may be able to match your client or campaigns with. Journalists who use this method are normally on quick deadlines, so you can often see successfully pitched content translate into links and coverage within hours!

6.3 Dynamic PR

Written by: Abigail Fairfoull

As we know too well, building brand awareness and credibility has always hinged on effective PR, a principle that remains unchanged in today's digital era. The shift from traditional avenues has now evolved into dynamic digital campaigns that have a wider online approach. Digital PR is constantly evolving and, to stay relevant, we must instil a dynamic PR strategy, to ensure that we are adaptive, responsive, and flexible to the ever-changing media landscape.

We recognise that in the dynamic realm of digital PR, harnessing real-time data, monitoring social media, and continually adapting communication strategies, are essential to align with the evolving needs and expectations of the audience.

How to Create a Dynamic PR Strategy

Let's face it, as digital PRs, we have a tough time these days. Achieving and maintaining relevance in such a competitive field is not always easy. To succeed, we must establish meaningful connections with journalists and deliver messaging that resonates with them. Today, as we adapt to the ever-evolving media landscape, PR extends way beyond traditional press releases and media pitches. As a digital PR agency, we employ various strategies to achieve impactful outcomes for our campaigns.

Creating Topical Stories Utilising Consumer Trend Data

Social media, in particular the video-sharing platform, *TikTok*, has brought about a paradigm shift in how we establish and maintain connections with the media and our target audience. *TikTok* has swiftly evolved into an integral element of our digital PR strategies. We utilise hashtag data and the popularity of current and upcoming trends, to create topical stories that appeal to the target audience, are relevant to our brand, and establish credibility and authority.

Whether we're pitching advice on how you can achieve the latest beauty trend, sparking conversation about the dangers of the latest '5 to 9' movement, or showcasing the bucket list travel destinations for the year ahead. We are constantly looking for the latest consumer trends that can help leverage coverage opportunities for the brands we work with.

You can successfully instil *TikTok* into your strategy, by doing the following:

- **Become Immersed in the Topics That Relate to Your Brand:** Whether you're working in beauty, health, or finance, *TikTok* is a source of information for all topics. Researching into these niche areas will give you insight into what your target audience is talking about and how topics of conversation are of interest to them at current.

- **Use Your Industry Knowledge to Inform a Story:** If you find a trend or story that is relevant to your brand, then use your expertise to offer further information that would appeal to your target audience. For instance, if you have expertise in mental health, you might provide advice on a dangerous wellness trend.

- **Support Your Insight with Credible Data:** It might sound obvious, but for a journalist to believe that a trend is a trend, there needs to be proof. Using *TikTok* hashtags and *Google* Trends data can help you back up your story, by showcasing a rise in popularity for a particular keyword or search term, like #lattemakeup or #girlmath.

- **Be Quick:** Trends have a really short life span — they can be around for sometimes as little as a week, before the next trend surfaces. So, you have to be quick. This type of story has the potential to be hugely successful, so this should take priority over other activities — make this a key focus for yourself and the team!

- **Diversify Your Content to Appeal to a Wider Audience:** Building links is hard. But we can learn a lot from our mistakes and use this to help fuel a dynamic strategy approach. The first failure that many PRs will encounter is not hitting the mark when trying to reach their target audience. Sometimes, the content that we think will fly, flops, and the one thing we have learnt, is to always look for extra opportunities. A lot of time and effort goes into creating a digital PR campaign, so the last thing you should do is give up if you aren't successful the first time around.

Through trial and error, what we have found is that sometimes, content can resonate with a different audience more than another. It's important during the development stage to discover new audience opportunities. By diversifying your content, you can reach a wider audience. An example of this could be, if you work in the healthcare industry, and you have created a story on how people in the workplace can reduce burnout during the summer holiday season. You can diversify this content to appeal to a mix of different, more niche audiences — for example, HR, retail, travel and more.

Monitor the News Cycle for Breaking News Stories

One thing we have learned since the pandemic is how influential the news cycle can be for digital PR. Covid-19, the cost of living crisis, Brexit, and more have all been used to create topical campaigns that have generated success for many brands. The key here is having that newsworthy hook that journalists want and need for a story to be published. After working with many brands in ultra-niche industries, we can appreciate that it can be hard to get journalists interested in a client's insight and expertise.

Now, there are a few criteria that need to be met, to ensure that even the niche topics can be successful in the news:

- **Timeliness:** This, in simpler terms, means that your campaign needs to be relevant to the news cycle right now. Whether that's talking about the current economic climate or consumer inflation — ensuring your content has that newsworthy hook is crucial to its success.
- **Geographical Relevance:** You can secure some great coverage by targeting hyper-local locations, through

specific city or regional data and stories. By closely monitoring the news cycle, you can use your expertise and brand insight to respond to local news.

- **Relevance:** The key to a successful strategy is ensuring that the content you are producing is relevant to your brand. What's important here is that your brand is credible enough to comment on the story and provide advice, tips, and guidance.

- **Fresh:** You don't want to waste your time creating a story that doesn't have a fresh and exciting spin on the news. The content needs to provide the journalist with a new take on the story that they haven't seen before, and would otherwise not be able to add themselves.

Research and Plan around Key Calendar Dates

While quick turnaround newsjacking stories are hugely successful, it's also important that when developing your dynamic PR strategy, you factor in long-lead stories.

Now, the most successful method we have found is planning campaigns around topical national holidays and key calendar dates like bank holidays, Christmas, and more. This can be anything from product suggestions for gift guides or expertise on specific topics.

Whether that's offering a journalist at *Glamour* your latest beauty product for a summer skincare round-up or advice on how you can save when travelling in peak season. Events like Valentine's Day, Black Friday, and Mother's Day all create the perfect opportunity to push your products or services as listed, and your in-house expertise.

We follow a simple method to achieving key forward-planning features:

- **Create a Calendar with Key Dates and Holidays:** From Blue Monday to National Croissant Day, there could be a weird and wonderful national awareness day or holiday that could be relevant to your brand. The idea of an event calendar is so that you can track these key dates for specific countries/regions.

- **Ideation for Specific Key Dates Far in Advance:** For the more obvious calendar dates like Mental Health Awareness Month and Christmas, there is a lot of competition, and it takes a lot to get cut through with journalists. So, preparation is key. Ahead of these events, schedule a brainstorming session to come up with fresh and exciting ideas.

- **Feature Pitching and Thought Leadership to Secure Features:** If you have a key calendar event coming up, this provides an opportunity to reach out to target publications to offer them exclusive tips, advice, and product review opportunities. In doing so, you can work collaboratively with journalists on exclusive stories.

Digital PR is a combination of many factors, as we explore in this book. However, what's important to understand is that to achieve a successful strategy, you must apply these different methods and create a dynamic PR strategy. This allows you to tackle individual objectives and reach your brand goals on a quicker scale.

6.4 Feature Pitching

Written by: Lauren Wilden

As digital PRs, we are tasked with the notoriously difficult job of securing clients high volumes of coverage and links within relevant publications — and it's becoming increasingly more difficult. Not only is the PR industry evolving at a rapid speed, but the world of online journalism has also had a turbulent few years. It's seen huge amounts of job cuts and editorial teams being restructured and streamlined.

This has understandably had a huge impact on the likelihood of more general pitches and outreach emails being seen, opened, and used by the time-restricted journalists, battling with their ever-growing inboxes. As a result, it's become increasingly necessary and effective to offer exclusive content to relevant journalists and publications we're striving to secure coverage with, on behalf of our clients.

What Is Feature Pitching?

A feature pitch is defined as an attempt to get a journalist, editor, or media outlet interested in your client's news, so that they decide to cover it as part of an exclusive or standalone story. As digital PRs working on behalf of a business or multiple clients, the goal is to integrate thought leadership. This comes in the form of expert commentary and — hopefully — links, as part of the coverage secured through this pitching technique.

Feature pitching is more of a traditional PR tactic. It can prove to be a great tool for securing links on niche sites. Especially ones that don't tend to run more commonly outreached data-led campaigns, reactive articles, and commentary pitched out widely to various outlets and publications.

As well as the SEO benefit of links being built via securing features, a well-targeted and relevant feature can also boost the reputation of a client or expert within their chosen field or industry. Essentially, giving them clout to share among industry peers on the likes of their website, *LinkedIn*, and *X* (formerly *Twitter*) profile.

It's important to bear in mind that feature pitching is not going to instantly produce results. It should ideally be undertaken alongside a mixture of reactive, newsroom, and hero campaign outreach, as required for the size and nature of a client base.

We focus on multiple types of feature pitching for clients across the B2C and B2B industries, these most commonly include...

A Thought Leadership Article Discussing an Industry Topic:	A CTO discussing how the introduction and technological advancements in AI are likely to impact the industry, in which this business operates in both the short and long term.
An Interview or Q&A Session on a Specific Topic:	A digestible breakdown of important information and insight from a client, on a relevant topic or industry update to build trust and authority for your client.
A Meet the Founder/CEO/Head of Article:	These are harder (but not impossible) to secure for smaller, less established clients. For example, meet the female business owner who quit her full-time job to embark upon a new journey focused on her true passion.
Exclusive Comments/Insight Alongside Other Industry Peers:	To assist with building brand awareness and establishing clients as 'ones to watch' within their field of expertise. E.g. providing exclusive industry insight and reaction to the autumn budget announcements.

What Kinds of Clients Are Likely to Benefit the Most from Feature Placements?

Often, we find that clients don't always appreciate just how newsworthy their insight and deep knowledge could be to journalists and publications. They may even feel like their experience doesn't constitute them being classed as an 'expert' in their field. You may also find, from delving into any previous press outreach efforts they've attempted, that they are focusing on hooks or angles that are much too promotional for organic pickup.

It's therefore vital for us as PRs to peel back the metaphorical layers and bridge the gap. This involves uncovering what clients have the ability and knowledge to offer publications, and pairing it with the newsworthy hooks and angles that journalists will be looking for. This will, in turn, create a compelling piece of content for their engaged audiences. Unfortunately, not all clients are going to be the strongest candidates for testing out feature pitching with.

What Are the Different Approaches Digital PRs Can Take When Feature Pitching for Clients?

As previously mentioned, feature pitching for new clients or existing clients within a new industry sector, can be a real trial and error process. We have to figure out, as PRs, where the appetite lies for the kinds of experts we're pitching exclusive commentary on behalf of.

That being said, there are a few pearls of wisdom that I've picked up during the past year of feature pitching for a subsection of our clients:

- **There Is Always an Increased Interest in Female Business Leaders/CEOs/Experts:** Many journalists and publications are — quite rightly — looking to offer a diverse and varied take on topics and industries from experts they speak with. As is unfortunately the case within the majority of industries, the positions of CEOs are primarily dominated by males. So, if you happen to work for, or with, a client that boasts a female founder, CEO, or other very senior position — journalists will be more likely to open your pitch and agree to a feature.

- **Angles Pitched That Go 'Against the Grain' or That Question a General Consensus, Secure Impressive Open Rates:** Journalists and publications don't want to be using comments and insight from individuals who are all saying the same things, but in different ways. They want to be able to look at differing opinions and points of view, and give their readers new ways to look at things from expert perspectives. If you have a client who feels particularly strongly or passionately about a topic that goes against the status quo, look at how their opinions could be pitched as a feature or article with relevant publications.

- **Send Your Pitches to News Desks and Editorial Teams Simultaneously:** This might seem a little overkill or even downright spammy to some. However, anyone working in digital PR in the current climate, knows how hard it can be to even get a journalist to open an email, let alone decide to cover your client. So why not cover all bases with a targeted feature pitch to give yourself — and your client — the best possible chance of results?

- **Try Alternating the Times of Day You Schedule Feature Pitches:** A lot of PRs tend to wrongly assume that the only way to approach journalists with pitches and press releases, is first thing in the morning before 10 am.

Personally, however, I have found that targeted pitches containing suggested articles and topics of interest our clients can exclusively provide for them, actually boast higher open rates and a greater chance of replies from publications. This can work better than those scheduled first thing, when they are, no doubt, being bombarded by hundreds of PRs all desperate for them to open their email pitches.

It's always best to ask yourself some important questions, regarding the client you're looking to implement outreach for:

Personal Use Tick Sheet	Yes	No
Does the client have expertise on topics/articles that are likely to resonate with your target list of dream publications?	☐	☐
What experience or industry credentials do they boast, which you can use to your advantage to make your outreach pitch stand out from the crowd?	☐	☐
Can any existing blog articles/podcasts/white papers written by the experts you're looking to pitch, be sent alongside your initial feature pitch? This will provide an example of their tone of voice and experience in different areas.	☐	☐
Does your client have a list of target publications and/or ideas of angles/articles that will give you a good starting point?	☐	☐
Are you pitching features or articles that nicely hook onto a current or trending topic, which journalists are continuing to look for fresh, unique, or controversial* takes on?	☐	☐

*Controversial: Opinions on behalf of clients that go against the typical consensus of a topic, work extremely well for securing placements exclusively. They're particularly great for businesses in competitive markets such as marketing, personal finance, and automotive.

How to Construct a Successful Feature Pitch?

As with any initial outreach pitches to journalists, the subject line you choose for your feature pitch is of the utmost importance. After all, if it doesn't immediately capture their interest and make them want to open and read further into your email, then your efforts will have gone to waste.

Keep the subject line short and to the point of what you're offering them, and be sure to start the subject line with the words **'EXCLUSIVE FOR [PUBLICATION]'.** This lets them know that you're specifically targeting them. It also shows that you aren't just trying your luck by sending a huge list of media contacts the same generic pitch, in the hopes that someone takes you up on the opportunity.

Some examples of previous subject lines that have been pitched and have resulted in coverage and links within top-tier, national news sites or niche and relevant industry publications:

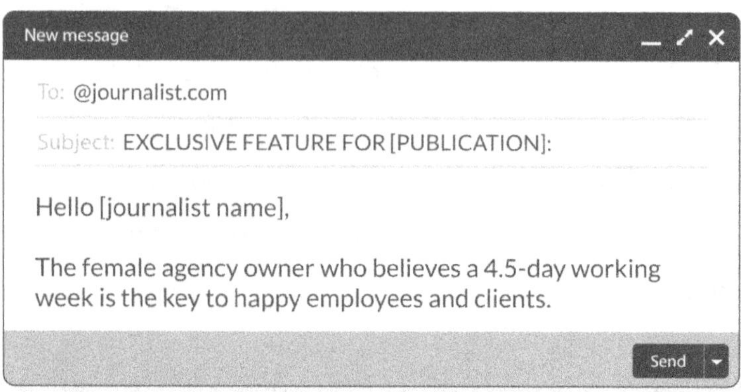
New message
To: @journalist.com
Subject: EXCLUSIVE FEATURE FOR [PUBLICATION]:
Hello [journalist name],
The female agency owner who believes a 4.5-day working week is the key to happy employees and clients.
Send

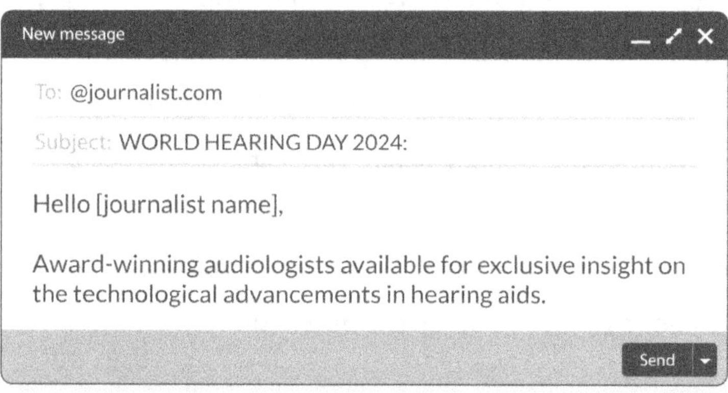
New message
To: @journalist.com
Subject: WORLD HEARING DAY 2024:
Hello [journalist name],
Award-winning audiologists available for exclusive insight on the technological advancements in hearing aids.
Send

New message
To: @journalist.com
Subject: EXCLUSIVE INTERVIEW OPPORTUNITY:
Hello [journalist name],
Founder of leading UK rehab centre shares how his own addiction experiences inspired his business journey.
Send

A checklist of things to remember when feature pitching for clients:

☐ Liaise with your clients to understand what expert insight/thought leadership they can offer. Make a wish list of their dream publications (phone calls/video chat work best for uncovering these potential hidden gems).

☐ Research relevant journalists and carry out extensive manual prospecting (freelancers/niche writers/feature editors/opinion editors).

☐ Track your outreach pitches, including where and when they were sent on a dedicated *Google* spreadsheet, to ensure there is no crossover in your work.

☐ Make sure you are aware of a publication's guidelines and the types of stories they will/won't accept, to avoid annoying any journalists with unnecessary emails.

☐ Consider how relevant a website is to your client's target audience/sector, and whether it's worth the time researching and writing an article. What DA/DR and online circulation are you looking at, AS WELL AS the target demographic?

☐ Always remember, feature pitching like this takes time and patience, so will a successfully secured feature/follow link on the site be beneficial in two or three months?

6.5 How to Leverage Internal Experts

Written by: Lauren Wilden

Digital PRs are often faced with a tricky challenge. Needing to immerse ourselves into a client's brand offering, while, at the same time, maintaining enough distance to effectively generate stories, campaigns, and hooks that will spark genuine interest among media publications and top-tier journalists.

One of the best ways to source newsworthy stories or features that will offer journalists something unique and fresh to cover, is via the client's in-house industry experts. This is an often untapped resource when it comes to digital PR. You never know what kind of hugely insightful experience, opinions, or advice an employee who has worked somewhere for several years may have on an emerging trend or planned campaign topic. OR just how beneficial this could be when securing dream publication coverage and links.

Utilising the in-house experts of clients that you are working with is a hugely powerful PR tactic. It can help to build brand awareness, and give a business more visibility and credibility among its competitors. Most notably, for digital PRs, it can help to build links to new and relevant referring domains, to help widen those all-important link gaps.

Why Are Experts So Important for Digital PR in the Current Climate?

A client's experts and in-house thought leaders, which you have access to, are a fantastic method of adding credibility and authority to a brand you've been tasked with building. It can also be particularly helpful for digital PRs finding it increasingly difficult to cut through the industry noise, and position themselves and the offerings of their clients in front of journalists.

The knowledge and experience of internal experts will enhance the trustworthiness and legitimacy of the content you're sharing with publications. It will also make it more appealing to the audiences that journalists are writing their articles and features for. The likelihood of content being shared with others, and across social media, increases when content has the backing of an industry field. This is because it further boosts the credibility of a brand and expands its awareness and loyalty to new and varied audiences.

How Can Digital PRs Make the Most Out of Internal Experts?

It may be the case that not all the clients that you and your team work with have suitable internal experts, able to offer up industry insight, reactions, and recommendations to publications and journalists you're looking to target. However, nine times out of ten, you will be able to utilise them for thought leadership comments.

Identify Your Client Experts

Whenever we are running an onboarding session for a new client, we always make sure that we source as much information as possible, on the various potential thought leaders within a company. We think about how they could be utilised for PR purposes, and for increasing all-important brand awareness. They may not consider themselves to be fully-fledged experts on certain topics or industries, but chances are they have a pool of untapped wisdom and experiences to share. This is perfect for helping to craft reactive comments for different angles.

Craft Compelling Pitches/Outreach Content

Your pitches and their accompanying email headlines/subject lines should highlight the expertise of your client's internal experts. Always make sure to highlight what your pitch/content is discussing, and that the email contains industry insight and reaction from an expert on the subject at hand.

Build Upon Ongoing Journalist Relationships

Trust and authenticity are not something that digital PR professionals can forge with journalists and publications within a client's industry overnight. It takes time and effort to be able to show the media why your internal experts offer valuable and meaningful advice, and knowledge on trending topics. Build upon relationships with key members of the press by offering them exclusives on insight from your client. Be sure to only target them with stories that you know they are likely to be covering, as part of the areas they cover. Once you start to see them approaching you for comments and reactions to stories — rather than the other way around — you will know your hard work is starting to pay off.

Monitor Industry Trends/Breaking News

As digital PRs, it's vital that we are able to stay abreast of industry trends and news. And that we have enough knowledge of the part that internal experts can play, in adding their own unique perspectives to thought leadership opportunities. Do they have opinions or points of view on different industry topics that you can monitor specifically? Can you create a Q&A bank of answers to general questions about their field of interest? This will help you further understand their TOV (tone of voice) and guide you when drafting up comments on their behalf.

Leverage Social Media

Use social media platforms to showcase the expertise of your client's internal experts. Encourage them to regularly share their insights through blogs, articles, or posts on their *LinkedIn*, *X* (formerly *Twitter*) or *TikTok* profiles. Establishing a digital footprint, can attract media attention from journalists and media outlets, looking for relevant people to speak to regarding certain industry topics.

6.6 Product Pitching

Written by: Lauren Wilden

While not all clients or brands will be able to benefit from product placements in the press, this traditional PR technique is a proven method that we've been implementing for several years. In its simplest terms, product placement PR (or product PR as we call it), aims to secure a business or brand's product or offering, a feature within the media.

Once audiences see publications, journalists, or bloggers reviewing and (hopefully) recommending the product(s), they will be incentivised to either visit the website and increase its organic traffic, or even make a purchase. There is also the longer-term benefit of product PR helping to establish brand awareness and ingrain a business or website in the minds of potential future customers.

What Are the Benefits of Product Pitching in Digital PR?

Product PR expands the coverage and link opportunities for clients looking to promote their offerings through news sites, blogs, TV shows, and even print titles their target demographics are consuming. We'd like to hope that data-led hero campaigns, well-timed proactive and reactive pieces, and newsjacking comments will be enough to secure coverage and links in dream publications. However, unfortunately, that's not always the case, and that's when we turn to product PR pitches.

It might be that your client has a burning desire to see their products featured on *BBC Good Food*, *The Guardian Online*, or even live on *ITV* in the consumer round-up segment, showcased on *This Morning*. These are all placements that the team here at JBH have secured over the past year for our clients, thanks to product pitching — and it's not as complicated or difficult as you might imagine.

What Can Digital PRs Do to Maximise the Chances of Product PR Coverage and Links?

If you work in marketing, you might have heard about brands planning for Christmas, as early on in the year as June or July. While this is also the case in traditional PR settings, with digital PR, we are lucky to have an abundance of tools at our disposal, to help share relevant products with journalists when search demand is at an all-time high.

For one of our clients, we were tasked with promoting their luxury 12-day Advent Cocktail box in the lead-up to December 1st. We wanted to make sure that our press outreach and email pitches that focused on its offerings, were sent at the best possible time for maximum impact and interest. Due to the product being deemed a luxury item, alongside the client having limited stock to sell due to them being produced in Italy. We were unable to offer journalists the opportunity to receive a sample of the advent box itself. However, we did convince the client to allow us to send target journalists and publications samples of some cocktails included in the box. We also sent across high-res imagery, product descriptions, and all the necessary information required to cover it should they wish.

Using *Google Trends*, we looked at specific search demand for the terms around 'Alcohol Advent Calendars' over the previous five years. We did this to determine the best possible time to start communicating with target journalists, regarding the client's festive offering. We could see a clear spike in search demand for the core phrases around the second and third week of November, so that's when the heavy emphasis on our product pitching commenced.

As a result of our efforts, we secured coverage, reviews, and (most importantly) links for our client on some dream target publications. This included *BBC Good Food, Delish, Olive Magazine, Time Out UK*, and many more. Also as a result of our product pitching efforts, *ITV's This Morning* shared the advent cocktail box to an *Instagram* audience of almost 3 million followers — driving further audience reach for the brand.

Following an abundance of articles and coverage going live, our client witnessed a huge spike in referral traffic to the product, and sold out of the item well before the start of December.

What Are the Drawbacks to Product PR to Be Aware Of?

Despite the fantastic coverage opportunities that can emerge from well-planned, strategised, and executed product PR pitching, there are certain things to take into consideration when it comes to suggesting it to your clients. That may mean it's not the best use of your time.

How Unique or Newsworthy Are the Products You're Able to Pitch?

It can be all too easy to get swept up in a client's passion and excitement for a particular product or range, which they are keen to promote to target audiences. While it's important, as PRs, to share their vision and beliefs, it's also vital that we stay realistic and offer genuine advice to our clients. This can include feeding back that we don't think something has a unique enough angle or hook, to be interesting enough for journalists to cover as a standalone story or among other industry competitors.

It might be that you can see better opportunities within another product your client boasts, which may result in wider coverage opportunities. Perhaps you think a pitch at a different time of the year, such as in the lead-up to Christmas, Easter, or Mother's Day, might be more successful in enticing journalists to cover a particular brand.

Don't be afraid to have honest conversations with clients, if you feel unsure about what they are asking of you. PRs aren't miracle workers, and free editorial coverage and reviews for products are very difficult to achieve in an extremely competitive market.

Has Your Client Got a Sufficient Budget for Journalist Gifting?

There are no guarantees that sending free products to journalists or bloggers will result in coverage. So, they need to understand this when agreeing to a monetary budget for you to use when pitching. You might successfully hear back from 20 journalists wanting to review or test out a product when sending out your initial pitches. However, this does NOT necessarily mean that it will result in 20 individual pieces of coverage or links. Journalists are well within their rights to accept the gift, and have absolutely no obligation to use it in their work.

That being said, we undertake a strict filtering process when creating bespoke media lists, to pitch our clients' products and services to. This ensures the best chances of secured coverage when sending out goods and products.

Is Your Client Prepared for Honest and Potentially Negative Articles?

On the rare occasions that we send out clients' products to journalists or publications that result in negative or less favourable reviews, there is, unfortunately, nothing we can do about this. This is because it's 100% based on the journalist's own feelings and thoughts about what they've received. Often, journalists will be transparent about this, and give us a heads-up about why they won't be recommending a product to their readers or will leave it out of an article altogether.

131

Occasionally, we've been able to rectify the situation. This involved sending the journalist an alternative offering on behalf of a client, which was received in a much more positive light. It's important to prepare clients that just because a journalist has said yes to receiving and reviewing their product, it might not be the glowing review they are hoping for.

Three top things to consider when pitching products for clients:

1. Timing is Everything

You might think you know when audiences are most likely to be interested in purchasing your client's products or services, but what data do you have to support this hunch? Implementing tools like *Google Trends, Google Glimpse,* or *BuzzSumo* will give you some real insight into when and where the demand spikes.

2. React Quickly If You Spot a Relevant Trend

Pop culture rules a lot of the news cycle. So, PRs looking to secure product reviews and coverage can certainly use this to their advantage. Spotting trends as they are on the cusp of emerging — but just before absolutely EVERYONE is talking about them — is a real art. Don't waste any time in reaching out to relevant sectors. If you see a trend that's relevant to your client being discussed on social media, it might just mean that you can get cut through on showcasing a particular product, before other competitors jump on the bandwagon.

3. Research Who You're Pitching To/Keep Media Lists Tight

Manual prospecting is key when it comes to identifying and testing out the very best places to pitch client products. Research the kinds of journalists (both freelance and editorial) at target publications, who have written up similar reviews or articles in the past.

Don't be afraid to use any public social media profiles to your advantage, to find any further insight or information on a writer you're pitching to — do they have a dog? Are they partial to a particular drink or alcohol brand? Are they particularly fond of certain fashion or beauty brands? All of this information will help you to draft a personalised and unique pitch that appeals specifically to them.

Chapter 7: Outreach

7.1 How to Write an Outreach Email and Follow-Ups

Written by: Abigail Fairfoull

Whether you've crafted a visually appealing infographic or uncovered compelling survey data, rest assured, there's likely someone eager to share it with their readers. Ensuring your content reaches the right audience is the most crucial element of effective digital PR. But knowing how to pitch, when to pitch, and who to pitch to can often feel like a minefield. The problem? The competition is intense, and journalists find themselves inundated with a barrage of press releases. Some receive upwards of 100 pitches a day from PR professionals. We have found that the most effective way to secure coverage is through the creation and delivery of a well-crafted media pitch. So, how exactly can you create a media pitch that grabs the interest of journalists?

Make Sure Your Pitch is Newsworthy

First and foremost, ask yourself, is your pitch newsworthy enough? To put it simply, Collins Dictionary says:

"Newsworthy is considered to be interesting enough to be reported in newspapers or on the radio or television."

Whether your story is considered newsworthy or not can determine if journalists will cover it. There are five points we follow to hit the criteria when pitching our stories:

1. The Timing Must Be Right

Whether you're responding to a breaking news story about the latest inflation report, or providing expert insight into the hottest new trend on *TikTok*, timing is very important. If your story is pitched too late, then it might be considered old news.

 **Top Tip**

To secure credible and valuable placements for your brand, you must have your finger on the pulse at all times. One way to make this easier is to set up Google alerts for key terms that relate to your industry. In doing so, you will know when relevant news breaks.

2. Decide if This Will Have an Impact

When it comes to newsworthiness, your target reach is important. If you can make your story appealing to a wider audience, this opens the possibility to target more publications and reach a wider audience, therefore increasing coverage.

> **Top Tip**
>
> Say you have created a piece on the importance of wellbeing at work, due to some statistics released by the NHS. Could your piece be adapted to reach more than just health publications? Could you tailor the content to make it appealing to niche sector publications?

3. Location, Location, Location

One factor that is often overlooked is the value of city-based and hyper-local news. If you can reach a smaller community with a story that resonates and is personal to them, you can heighten news relevance, i.e. newsworthiness.

4. Find Conflict and Controversy

One thing readers love is a dispute, whether it be about the latest reality TV program, a royal mishap, or a government announcement. Strong opinions, which highlight that someone is in disagreement with a certain narrative, provide a great story.

> **Top Tip**
>
> While it's great to be daring when it comes to PR, it's always important to tread with caution. The opinions you share should NOT cause any offence and should merely be offering a counterargument. One place to start could be debunking a common hack.

5. Weird and Wonderful News

Now, as we all know too well, the weird and wonderful things we see online have a way of bringing us back in for more. Whether it be a pimple-popping video or the latest *TikTok* challenge — unusual PR stories always have great success!

Create the Perfect Pitch Format

Journalists are bombarded with email pitches and press releases daily, which means getting your story noticed and covered is even more challenging. Remember, in today's PR, most journalists, and bloggers prefer not to be contacted via phone. They rely solely on your pitch, which means making your email stand out is crucial to securing coverage for your client.

There are certain steps you can take to create the 'perfect pitch' that we follow, which you can replicate for your own stories:

Give Them a Glimpse of Your Story in the Subject Line

You want to keep in mind that the subject line is where you make your first impression. So, to make sure your pitch is seen and not dumped straight into the bin, make sure your subject line gives detail into exactly what your story includes and what they can expect to receive. Here are some examples of good subject lines that hit the criteria:

> *Exclusive Interview: Mental Health Nurse on Reducing Burnout in the Workplace*

> *Survey Finds That 53% of Brits are Holidaying in the UK Instead of Travelling Abroad*

> *Dog Behaviourist Shares Advice to Pet Parents on How to Walk Your Dog in Winter*

> *New Product Alert: Floral Gin Released for Spring 2024*

You don't want your pitch to get lost behind puns and fancy jargon, instead, keep it short and sweet. Further down in your pitch is where you can provide more in-depth information.

Be Concise and Straight to the Point

Journalists don't have a lot of time on their hands, so don't beat around the bush – get straight to the story. In your introduction, you need to use as few words as possible to tell them exactly: Who, What, When, Where and Why? The top line is your opportunity to give the recipient a condensed overview of exactly what you are offering. This includes what your story is about, the most interesting elements of your story, and the angle that is most likely to catch the attention of the journalist.

Give Them Detailed Insight

Now what's important — and this is especially key when pitching a story, or providing quick turnaround content in response to breaking news — is to give the journalist everything they will need for their story. Whether that's key information, a quote from an expert, or some topline information about your client's brand. Journalists need to have all information readily available, so they can turn their story around quickly.

Let Them Know How They Can Find More Information

The purpose of your pitch should be to provide as much information to the recipient as possible, to increase your success in securing coverage. Within your pitch, you should include:

- **Links to Relevant External Sources**: Whether that's a recent campaign, the latest product listed on the site, or in-depth information about an in-house expert.

- **Contact Details:** This might seem obvious, but it can sometimes be overlooked. You must provide your contact details, including email, phone number, and company number, so that a journalist can contact you in a method that is suitable to them.

- **The Additional Information You Can Offer:** While your story might not fit with what the journalist is currently writing about, you should always offer the additional services and information the brand or in-house expert can provide.

Top Tip

Your pitch should be condensed into a digestible format, so that the reader can take the relevant information needed and not lose interest. That's why it's important to ensure that you are targeting the right information to the right audience.

Make Your Email Personalised to Each Journalist

It's important to make sure our emails stand out, and one quick and easy way to do this is by personalising your media pitches to each journalist or blogger. It is easy for recipients to recognise large batch-sent emails, and they are often directly thrown into the bin. By adding a subtle yet distinctive element within the story to make it feel personalised to the journalist, you can ensure that your pitch stands out against the others.

You can start by adding a touch of personalisation into the subject line, and this can be as simple as *'Exclusive for {publication} on burnout during winter'*. This shows the journalist that your pitch has been tailored to their title from the get-go, and that you are willing to go above and beyond to provide them with the information they need to write such a story.

It's easy to add subtle elements of personalisation throughout your pitch, while also trying to establish a relationship with the writer. One effective way to do this is by showing them that you have read previous articles that they have published. For example...

This demonstrates to the journalist that you read articles they have written. It also shows you have a solid understanding of their role within the publication, as well as the topics that they are interested in covering. One way to take this a step further is to comment on something interesting they have reported on within the piece, for example...

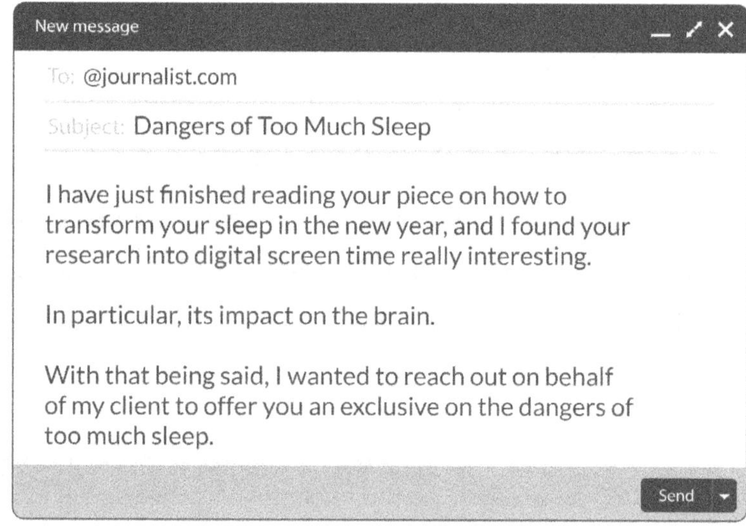

This shows the journalist that you are really interested in their work and that you believe your brand can provide them with a story that resonates with their target audience. When including reference to content, make sure that the information you are providing is either relevant to their previous work or an interesting take on an existing story — or a fresh story altogether. Finally, that it is in fitting with the publication they write for and their readers. As PRs, one of the most important, but often overlooked, responsibilities within our roles, is to establish relationships with journalists and bloggers.

It's all about getting your client's name and brand recognised in their inbox. You can start doing this by:

- Following the journalist/blogger on their work X (formerly *Twitter*) account.
- Engaging with their posts that resonate with your client's brand/offering.
- Providing positive feedback and comments on their published stories.

> **Top Tip**
>
> If you have previously worked with a journalist, reach out to them in the same email chain. This way you can continue building this relationship and assure them that you have an understanding of their target reader and their story offerings.

Find the Right PR Pitch for Your Story

Outreach isn't a one-size-fits-all approach. You need to be able to tailor the way you pitch depending on the type of content, the publication, and the journalist you are targeting. Being adaptable is important within our roles as digital PRs, and understanding the different requirements of publications is crucial to your success in securing coverage for your brand. There are certain key characteristics you need to determine before you start writing your pitch. These include understanding your audience and who you are trying to reach, the tone of voice and format of your pitch, and finally what type of content you are pitching.

These specific elements will determine what type of pitch format you should replicate:

Breaking News Pitch

If you are pitching a story that responds to a breaking news story, then your pitch should include all the information that the journalist would need to turn the story around quickly. Plus, insight into exactly what trending story you are responding to.

Collaborative Pitch

When working on a long-lead story through feature pitching and thought leadership, you would format a collaborative pitch. This would include in-depth insight into your client's brand, the service they offer, and how they can collaborate with the journalist for a story. For this type of pitch to be successful, you should include a selection of story ideas that you can help provide research, exclusive commentary, interviews, and more for the journalist.

Exclusive Pitch

The same principle applies here. When working on an exclusive pitch, you need to give the reader an in-depth understanding of exactly what you can provide to the journalist and why you think this will be insightful for their target audience. This is a long-lead method of PR that helps us to target journalists at higher authority publications like *The Telegraph* and *The Guardian*.

Product Review

Your product pitch should avoid any sales and marketing language, this should be offering a collaborative approach with the brand. It should provide the journalist with adequate information on the product launch, offering, and key statistics.

Reactive Pitch

A reactive pitch should always provide the journalist with all the information they need to fulfil their piece. This includes tips, expert commentary, and research findings. It should give the recipient a glimpse into why this is trending right now and what makes it relevant to their target audience — this can be done by adding consumer data.

7.2 Media List Creation and Media Databases

Written by: Abigail Fairfoull

If we have a look at exactly what it takes to generate great coverage for your brand, the digital PR formula comprises the following elements:

- A compelling and newsworthy story.
- A meticulously curated media list featuring key journalists.
- A tailored pitch that aligns with the story and resonates with the targeted journalists.

While there can be overriding factors (out of your control), which can influence the results generated from your pitch, these three key elements are the structure to success. As a professional in the PR space, you will understand that a strong media list is essential in ensuring that your story is placed in front of the right journalists, at the relevant publications for your brand. This can make the process of curating a press list somewhat challenging and time-consuming.

However, creating a well-constructed media list is integral to the success of your campaign, and is key to ensuring your brand is featured in the right publications. After all, if you've spent time crafting a great piece of content, then you want to ensure that your pitch is sent to the right target audience, who will be likely to cover your story.

What Is a Media List in Digital PR?

A media list, otherwise known as a press list, is a record of contacts, including journalists and bloggers. They are grouped by similarities, which can often include location, media type (digital, print, radio, and television), the topics covered, and writing specialities (including e-commerce, SEO and more). These lists typically include important information such as names, job titles, contact information, media organisations and topics of interest. Many PRs will be all too familiar with a media list, but the difficulty comes from knowing exactly how to create one that will have the most value for your client.

How to Build a Media List?

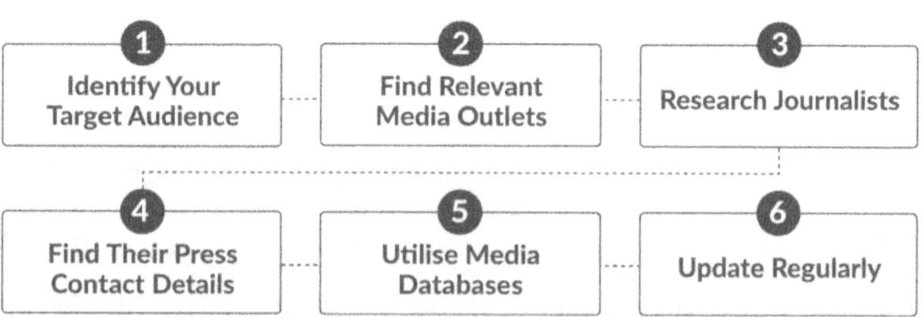

1. Identify Your Target Audience

The first step in curating a media list is identifying your target audience. You should already have an understanding of whom the main audience is for your client. But now you need to discover what they are interested in, what types of media they engage with, and their key defining traits. This insight will help you discover exactly what types of publications you should be targeting, and your style of pitching, to help generate the best results. Social media is a great tool to source this information, as you can see exactly what your target audience is talking about, what they find interesting, and what they are engaging with.

2. Find Relevant Media Outlets

Once you have a full understanding of who you are trying to reach, you will be able to create a list of credible publications to target. Often, when researching relevant media outlets to target, many will limit their search to the high domain sites like *The Telegraph*, *Glamour*, *Cosmopolitan* and more. However, what's important to note is that smaller domain sites that are relevant to your brand and target audience, can hold significant value for digital PR activity. Use *Google* search, social media, and your selected media database to find sites that are in fitting with the content within your pitch. Whether it's an industry-specific publication that covers health and wellbeing content, a beauty publication dedicated to product reviews, or an informational fleet site that covers content centred around electric vehicles.

3. Research Journalists

Start by looking for journalists who have covered similar topics to those you are pitching about. Alternatively, look for journalists who work within specific industries that are relevant to your brand. You can use *Google News* and *X* (formerly *Twitter*) to discover the writers who specialise in your field — these are likely the people who will be interested in publishing your story. Use keywords and phrases that relate to your client's brand and the story that you are pitching. *Google News* search will flag up any journalists who have recently covered stories that relate to your chosen topics. If you think they are a relevant fit, they can be added to your list.

4. Find Their Press Contact Details

There are numerous ways you can find a journalist or blogger's contact information. The first and most obvious is using a media database that stores information on each writer, including their email address, topics covered, and preferred method of contact. Now, sometimes, the information is unavailable on a media database, and this is when building a press list becomes more complex and time-consuming. But fear not, social media is a great tool that can speed up the process. Journalists will often leave their contact details in their social bios, especially on *TikTok*, so do a quick search for them on the app.

Top Tip

If a journalist's contact details are not listed in their X (formerly Twitter) bio, copy their user @ and paste it directly into the search bar, followed by 'email'. If they have shared their email previously on the app then this should flag up for you - it's quick and simple!

5. Utilise Media Databases

Media databases like *Muck Rack*, *Roxhill*, *Prowly* or similar tools, will become your best friends when creating media lists for outreach. They are the quickest and easiest way to find contact information for journalists and bloggers, writing for some top publications. We recommend trialling several media databases before you commit to just one, as each tool has its own system and ways of working that might be more suitable for you.

6. Update Regularly

One of the most important things that needs to be done when curating a media list, is to make sure that you update the contact information regularly. Often, journalists will move to a different publication, and their roles and the topics they cover may change — so it's important to consistently monitor journalists' social media and recent articles for any changes.

It is incredibly valuable to note that when pitching to the press, you create a bespoke media list for each pitch you send. Through research, you may discover more journalists writing about similar topics, who will be interested in your story.

Tips for Building a Solid Media List

1. Find Geographical Relevance

This is particularly important when building press lists. You should always specify the region, city, and country in which the writer lives, and if they write for a specific location publication, for instance, the *New York Post*. This information is important in ensuring you are targeting content to the most relevant audience.

2. Take a Quality Over Quantity Approach

Make sure the journalists and bloggers you are including within your list are relevant to your client and cover similar topics to what you are pitching. The last thing you want to do, as a PR, is send irrelevant content and damage your relationship with journalists.

3. Monitor Coverage Generated by Your Competitors

It's likely that if a journalist is interested in writing content produced by brands working within a similar field, then they will be open to receiving pitches from your client.

4. Network

To establish a relationship with journalists before pitching, attend industry gatherings, conferences, and networking events to connect with others. You can start to build credibility and cultivate relationships over time.

5. **Set *Google* Alert Notifications for Key Phrases that Link to Your Client and Your Pitch**

Whether it's 'new beauty trend', 'NHS mental health', or 'inflation rates', you can see daily which new journalists are writing about your chosen topics.

7.3 International Outreach

Written by: Sophie Clinton

Digital PR is experiencing significant growth, not only in the UK but on a global scale. Numerous clients seek agencies capable of meeting their coverage requirements at both national and international levels.

The Essence of International Outreach

International outreach in digital PR refers to the strategy of pitching content to journalists outside your home country, with the hope that your press release will be featured in their publications. This approach is not just about expanding reach; it's a form of engagement that requires cultural sensitivity, an understanding of diverse media landscapes, and an ability to tailor messages to various audiences.

Why International Outreach Matters

The digital world knows no borders. Leveraging international media channels can significantly amplify a brand's message, bringing about unparalleled visibility and credibility. As David Meerman Scott, a marketing strategist, aptly puts it, "In the age of the web, you are what you publish". Your content's international reach can redefine your brand's narrative on a global stage.

Understanding the Global Media Landscape

The key to successful international outreach lies in understanding the diverse global media landscape. Each country has its own unique media culture, preferences, and practices. What works in the UK might not resonate in Germany or Japan. It requires meticulous research, keen cultural insights, and often, collaboration with local PR professionals who can provide invaluable, on-ground perspectives.

Promoting information internationally and attempting to achieve widespread reach poses unique challenges. Irrespective of location or language, it might seem daunting — but it doesn't necessarily require being a corporate giant. In truth, securing international links follows a similar fundamental process as obtaining coverage at the national and regional levels in the UK.

Yet, to achieve success, four essential steps must be taken — and you must start at the very beginning from ideation, through to data, design, and outreach strategy:

1. Ideation

Obtaining international links begins right from the initial stages, especially when you have a client seeking specific links in regions such as the US or Europe. The first crucial step involves an extensive brainstorming session to generate ideas, concepts, and campaigns that are intricately tailored to the target locations. In this phase, it's essential to delve into the unique characteristics, preferences, and trends of the international audience you are targeting. Understanding the cultural nuances and market dynamics of each region is vital for crafting campaigns that resonate effectively. Whether it's the diverse consumer behaviours in the US or the multilingual landscape in Europe, a tailored approach is key.

Once you have a comprehensive understanding of the target locations, you can develop campaigns that not only align with the client's goals, but also integrate seamlessly with the local context. This might involve adapting content, messaging, or promotional strategies to ensure cultural relevance and resonance. By prioritising location-specific considerations from the outset and tailoring your approach accordingly, you set the foundation for a successful international digital PR campaign that effectively reaches and engages the desired audience.

2. Data

Once you have pinpointed a concept that focuses on the specific locations your client wants to secure links in, the next step is to collect the campaign data. It is important to ensure that the data is factually accurate and that you are utilising studies and statistics from the specific locations. This step is pivotal in crafting content that resonates authentically with the chosen international audiences. Accuracy is paramount during the data collection process. It's imperative to source information from reputable studies, industry reports, and relevant statistical sources specific to the targeted locations. By leveraging data derived directly from the regions in question, you ensure the factual integrity of your campaign, bolstering its credibility and relevance.

Meticulously collecting factually accurate and region-specific data lays the groundwork for a successful digital PR campaign. One that not only meets, but surpasses, the unique demands and expectations of your client in the chosen international destinations.

3. Design

To enhance the visual appeal and effectiveness of your outreach pitches in a multi-country or multi-city campaign, consider integrating designs that highlight each specific location you are targeting with key angles. Maps and index tables emerge as powerful assets in this scenario, offering a visually engaging and informative element to your outreach materials. Start by creating customised designs that visually represent each country or city you are focusing on. Utilise maps to pinpoint geographical locations, and use different colour schemes to differentiate between various regions. This not only enhances the aesthetic appeal of your pitches, but also provides a quick and intuitive understanding of the campaign's geographic scope.

Integrate index tables that outline key angles or aspects relevant to each location. This could include demographic information, unique cultural features, or specific market trends. Organising data in a clear and accessible format through index tables adds a professional and structured dimension to your outreach materials. These visual elements become invaluable in email pitches, as they serve as compelling visual aids that can capture the attention of your audience swiftly.

4. Content and Outreach

As your idea or campaign progresses to the outreach stage, it becomes crucial to tailor materials and assets specific to each country or city you are targeting. Develop individual pitches and press releases dedicated to highlighting the unique strengths or accomplishments of each location. This creates a personalised 'this is what your city/country excels at' style of presentation. Consider the impact of offering journalists content and press releases in their native language. Translating email pitches and press releases while incorporating relevant angles for the target markets, significantly enhances your chances of success. This personalised approach not only demonstrates cultural sensitivity, but also ensures that your messaging resonates effectively with local media outlets.

Stay attuned to the distinct characteristics of each country, including festivities, bank holidays, and awareness days. Align your campaign with ongoing events or relevant dates to maximise its impact and relevance in the local news landscape. Connecting your campaign to specific events can amplify its newsworthiness and capture the attention of journalists covering related topics.

To truly make an impact, go beyond generalised outreach and engage in personalised communication. Reach out to individual journalists and bloggers, establishing a relatable connection. By demonstrating a genuine understanding of their interests and preferences, you increase the likelihood of your content reaching the right audience and gaining the attention it deserves. In the realm of international outreach, going big means going personal. Taking the time to connect with individual journalists on a more personal level ensures that your campaign stands out amidst the noise and resonates effectively within diverse media landscapes.

Top Tips for US Outreach

Securing links from the US can be trickier. However, breaking your campaigns/content/pitches/strategy down by state or city can give you more chance of success:

- **Targeting US Links:** Securing links from the US can be challenging. Breaking down campaigns, content, pitches, and strategies by state or city can enhance success rates.

- **Regional Focus:** Instead of relying solely on broad topics like lifestyle or interiors, consider targeting regional and national news journalists. Break target lists down by state and/or city, aligning with the specific focus of your campaign or content.

- **Topical and Newsworthy:** Success with this tactic is dependent on having topical and newsworthy content or campaigns. Ensure that your outreach pitch is highly relevant and resonates with the interests of the targeted regions.

- **Awareness of News Cycle:** Stay up to date on the current news cycle and media landscape. Timing is crucial; pitch your campaigns when they align with the prevailing interests and trends in specific countries, cities, states, or regions.

- **Adaptability:** Be adaptable to changes in the media environment. Tailor your approach based on the dynamic nature of news cycles and evolving interests within the targeted geographical areas.

- **Strategic Pitching:** Break down your strategy to be state or city-specific, optimising your chances of success in different locales. Consider the uniqueness of each region and tailor your pitches accordingly. Recognise that a one-size-fits-all approach may not be effective and customise your outreach strategy based on regional characteristics.

- **Evaluation of Content Relevance:** Evaluate the relevance of your content or campaign to specific regions before pitching. Ensure that your messaging aligns with the preferences and priorities of the targeted states or cities.

7.4 How to Ask for a Link

Written by: Sophie Clinton

In the fast-paced world of digital PR, the ability to secure a hyperlink from a journalist is a nuanced and critical skill. This process goes beyond mere content promotion; it requires a strategic understanding of a journalist's needs, the art of crafting compelling pitches, and the ethical considerations inherent to media relations.

Understanding the Journalist's Perspective

Journalists are inundated with pitches and press releases. Your email has to stand out to catch their attention. Simon Read from *BBC* emphasises the importance of an email's headline, suggesting, "It should convey the topicality and worthiness of the content in just four or five words, given the extremely limited time a journalist might spend on each email". This insight underscores the need for conciseness and relevance in your approach.

Tomé Morrissy-Swan from *The Telegraph* highlights the advantage of having a pre-existing relationship with the journalist and tailoring the subject line to their beat or interest. This suggests that relationship building is as crucial as the content of your pitch.

I think all of us in the digital PR industry have experienced the pain of an unlinked brand mention on countless occasions. Yes, your client has been mentioned, and yes, the content was credited back to your client — but sadly, your precious, juicy link is nowhere to be found.

Thankfully, there's a simple solution to these unlinked brand mentions — just ask for the link! Having already mentioned your brand or client, it's clear that the journalist finds value in your content, and wants to share that value with their audience. This puts you in a great position to ask for the cherry on top. To help with this process, I also have a chaser email formula — backed by a Creative Commons (CC) licence — that can sometimes be more persuasive to get journalists to convert that mention into the desired link.

But before we get to that, let's start with the basics:

First, the Low Down... What Are Unlinked Brand Mentions?

Unlinked brand mentions are online mentions (citations) of your brand, or anything directly related to your brand, which do not link back to your site. Once identified, you can contact the website or journalist, and request that the mention of your brand be referenced with a backlink supplied back to your website.

Here's an example for JBH:

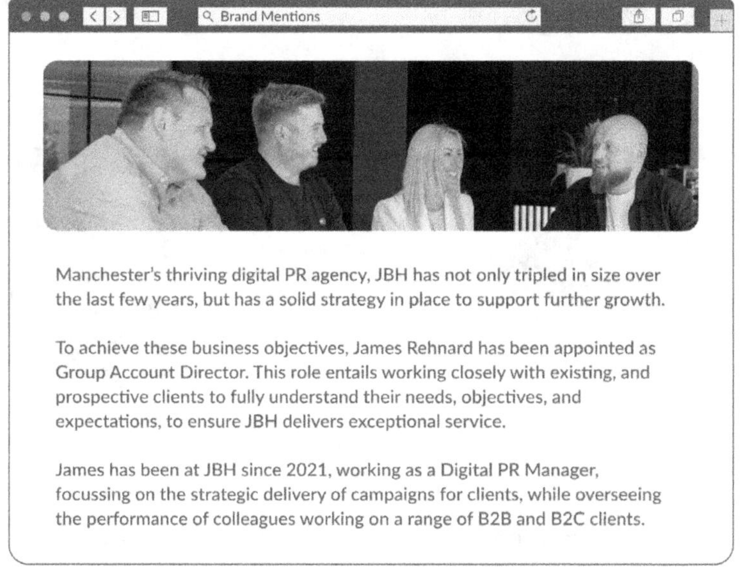

Manchester's thriving digital PR agency, JBH has not only tripled in size over the last few years, but has a solid strategy in place to support further growth.

To achieve these business objectives, James Rehnard has been appointed as Group Account Director. This role entails working closely with existing, and prospective clients to fully understand their needs, objectives, and expectations, to ensure JBH delivers exceptional service.

James has been at JBH since 2021, working as a Digital PR Manager, focussing on the strategic delivery of campaigns for clients, while overseeing the performance of colleagues working on a range of B2B and B2C clients.

You can see that despite the article citing JBH, there's no link back to our website. Earning a brand mention on a news site is the halfway point to earning a linked piece of coverage for your client or brand. You know that the author has covered your content/research, so they're familiar with your client or brand — giving you the perfect excuse to reach out and, hopefully, convince them to convert that mention into a link.

Here's an example with the link included:

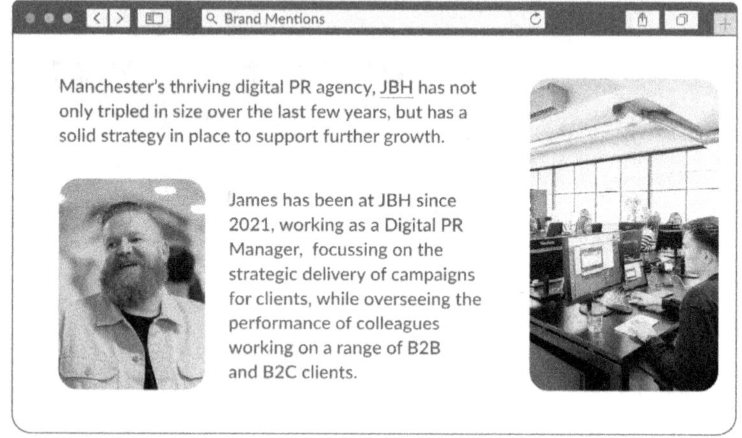

Are you creating valuable content but not getting credit where it's due? Here's my step-by-step process for turning unlinked client mentions into links:

1. Scan the Web for Unlinked Mentions of Your Brand/Client

The first step is to scan the web for any unlinked mentions of your brand or client. My favourite tools for this are *AHREFS, SEMRUSH, Talkwalker Alerts*, and *Google Alerts*. Once you've compiled a list of unlinked mentions, you must prioritise based on the highest SEO or PR value. If you have a well-established brand or client, you might find tons of unlinked mentions. Though you can manually attempt to capture a link on all of these websites, the best tactic is to prioritise the most authoritative websites that are going to add the most value to your client and their target demographic.

2. Find the Journalist's Contact Information

The ideal person to contact is the original author of the article. This can be found on the site's contact page, or by searching for them on software databases such as *Vuelio*, *Muck Rack*, *BuzzStream*, *Roxhill*, and *Prowly*.

 **Top Tip**

You can also use LinkedIn to search for the article's author or someone in a related position. If you're unable to find the author's email address, or the contact details for someone in their team, use the general information email or standard contact form.

3. The Pitch

Find a reason for the journalist to take the time and effort to insert a link. Word your request in a way that they can clearly see that linking to your client's website will not only benefit your client, but also provide value to them and their audience. Sometimes, internal pages are easier to link to than your client's homepage. For example, if there's a report, campaign, or case study page that covers the topic of discussion that you're trying to acquire a backlink on, it might make more sense to request a link to that specific page instead. When asking for the link, be cordial and thank them for their time — avoid coming across as pushy. If it's an article, compliment it in a unique and genuine way. Also, be sure to thank them for including your client in the article.

Tips for Getting a Positive Response to a Link Reclamation Email

- Don't be (too) pushy.
- Use your common sense, and don't pursue every opportunity you come across.
- Pick your battles wisely and try not to annoy journalists. Remember to build relationships, not destroy them.

Writing Your Chaser Email

- Use the title of the article in the subject line.
- Say thanks — the journalist wasn't obligated to share your content, so don't forget this when asking them for a link.
- Be clear about where you want them to link.

- It might help to show an example of a publisher linking out correctly. This makes it clear what you mean by your link request email.

Chaser Email Example

The Untapped Magic of a Creative Commons Link Reclamation Email

As mentioned at the beginning of this chapter, the chaser email formula that I've found to maximise my link reclamation rate includes a Creative Commons (CC) licence.

A CC licence helps you to retain copyright, while allowing others to copy, distribute, and make use of your content — all while ensuring that you'll be credited appropriately. Most journalists will quickly recognise a CC licence when they come across one, which makes CCs truly invaluable for successful link reclamation.

Creative Commons Chaser Email Example

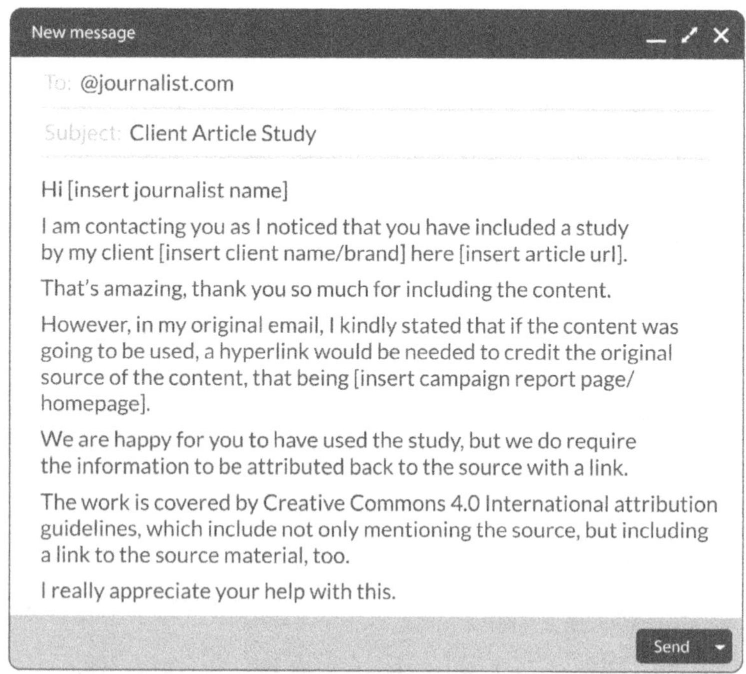

Here's an example of the CC licence being added to the footer of a client's landing page:

There are multiple CC licences to pick from, depending on what it is that you want to allow others to do with your content. The one we use at JBH is Creative Commons Licence 4.0 International. This states that publishers can share and/or adapt the material, as long as they credit the creator with a link back to the material. A CC is a great resource to have up your sleeve. Personally, I've found that my link reclamation conversion rate has been around 70% when CC licence rules are included in my chaser emails.

What to Do if the Answer Is Still 'No'?

At any point throughout this process, you might receive a negative response to your request. Sadly, there is no foolproof magic email template that'll change company policy or journalist/editor preference, when it comes to linking out to external sites. Therefore, in these cases, you need to take 'No' for an answer. Otherwise, you risk damaging your relationship with the journalist, and as any experienced digital PR knows, a friendly rapport between journalist and publication can be equally important as a link.

Key Takeaways for Link Reclamation

- Outline a reason that it would benefit the journalist to insert a link on your behalf.
- Use the title of the article in the subject line, so the journalist immediately knows what the email is regarding.
- Don't be (too) pushy.
- Use your common sense, and don't pursue every opportunity you come across.
- Pick your battles wisely — try not to annoy journalists. The goal is to build relationships, not destroy them.
- Be clear about the page you want them to link to — it might help to show an example of a publisher linking out correctly to demonstrate what you mean.
- Include a Creative Commons (CC) licence within chaser pitch emails to improve link reclamation success rate.
- Say thanks — remember, the journalist didn't need to share your content. Hopefully, you'll create a long-standing relationship!

Chapter 8: Measurement and Performance

8.1 Popular KPIs — What KPIs Should You Set for Digital PR?

Written by: Lauren Henley

Relevance

We all know that not all links are good links, but the best links are the most relevant ones. All work undertaken needs to reflect your brand and speak to your audience, therefore, relevance should be a key consideration.

Rankings and Organic Traffic

When you embark on SEO for your website, the ultimate goal is to climb the ranks in search engines and attract more visitors. Digital PR for SEO should follow the same principle. The focus? Elevate your ranking positions for relevant keywords, resulting in a surge of organic traffic. However, attributing better rankings and increased visitors solely to digital PR can be tricky. Various SEO activities could contribute to improvements. Yet, over time, your numbers should be on an upward trajectory. If not, it's time to reevaluate your SEO and digital PR strategies.

Referral Traffic

Referral traffic is a direct outcome you can attribute to your digital PR efforts. These are the visitors who arrive at your site by clicking on a backlink. Check this in *Google Analytics*, focusing on metrics like bounce rate and session duration. These indicators reflect the relevance and quality of a link.

Conversions

Digital PR isn't just about better rankings and increased traffic — it's about boosting sales. Track conversions by setting up specific goals in *Google Analytics*. Whether it's a newsletter signup, price enquiry, or purchase, tie these numbers back to each link and overall organic traffic.

Brand Awareness

In the race for links, brand awareness often takes a back seat. Yet, traditional PR aims for just that. Measure unlinked brand mentions, social media signals, and share of search to gauge brand awareness.

Recently, I was posed with a question...

"If you had to pick just three metrics to track in today's landscape, what would they be?"

In challenging economic times, proving your worth is non-negotiable. You've got to validate your contributions, providing insights that go beyond the surface. And while you're busy boosting a brand's digital PR, peeking into their analytics can unlock extra perks. It's not just about organic or referral traffic. You might spot opportunities to spice up their overall marketing game with trends around products or peaks in traffic from new channels.

In times of economic turbulence, the pressure to justify your value amps up. A recent (2023) Gartner study revealed that, '71% of CMOs are scraping by without the budget needed for their grand strategies'. That leaves us, the PR pros, with the job of proving our worth. So, in this ever-evolving digital PR scene, which metrics truly unlock the secret to showcasing value?

Volume of Coverage

Why? This metric can be tied to output — it shows how and why pitches are working. If you're reading this while grappling with a towering 'volume of coverage' KPI, relax. This advice comes with a few asterisks. In our recent survey with *PR Week*, we asked folks about their go-to metrics for PR impact. The resounding winner was the volume of coverage, with a whopping 71% making it their top PR measurement metric. Shocking? Maybe. Surprising? Not really. The obsession with link numbers and coverage quantity still looms large, overshadowing the crucial elements of quality and relevance. We've been in situations where we lost out on pitches because our projected link count wasn't as sky-high as the competition. But here's the reality — more coverage doesn't always mean more value. Let's dodge the race to the bottom that heaps pressure on PRs and delivers less bang for our client's buck. Remember, valuable coverage is the one that matters. Quantity metrics need a sidekick in the form of quality equivalents like sentiment, relevance, or engagement.

We've even created our own internal relevance metric to rate each piece of coverage. And don't forget, volume goals should dance to the tune of your industry. Pitching a mainstream beauty product? Your relevant coverage potential may genuinely be sky-high. But in healthcare, where space is tight, it's about reaching the right decision-makers. Showcasing the value of your coverage?

Compare and contrast the volume with metrics like sentiment or engagement. Prove that your coverage isn't just there; it's noticed. We've all seen those campaigns that bag loads of links but cause brand controversy. On paper, they seem like a hit, but a deeper look reveals potential long-term damage. Ten pieces of coverage that build your brand and boost relevance should beat hundreds that only add links to your backlink profile.

Relevant Traffic

Why? If content is king, then relevance is the queen. As PRs, we know building a brand is a marathon, not a sprint. Unlike PPC, tying our work to tangible outcomes isn't always a walk in the park. Crafting a clear strategy based on your brand's key targets reveals where your digital PR can make waves. "Build 100 links to a website" isn't a goal; it's an objective. Understanding the goal driving that objective, and the ways to create added value, becomes crystal clear.

Reporting that you've gained five pieces of coverage, leading to a spike in referral traffic, conversions, and sales? Now, that's the golden nugget. Digging into traffic details unveils engagement metrics and visitor time spent – painting a picture of what your target audience actually is and the sweet spots for valuable coverage. If your PR goals lean towards brand building, log the big campaign dates in analytics and track traffic spikes afterwards. After all, the common PR goal is to increase brand awareness and engagement. Traffic is the ticket to show off both. Understanding website traffic trends isn't just about bragging rights. In a downturn, it's your early-warning system — if your big campaign isn't making waves, real-time data lets you pivot.

Share of Search

Why? This proves that your work is building awareness of the brand. Enter share of search, a newer metric that we've used in reporting at JBH since December 2022. Over time, it reveals how much online visibility and search demand a brand gets compared to rivals. In the short term, it shows how vital starting PR work is for a brand. Calculated by monthly searches for relevant branded terms, share of search shows the ebb and flow of searches over a year of PR work.

This metric is gold because it doesn't just validate great coverage and immediate reader reactions through traffic — it shouts that a brand is steadily growing over time. Share of voice (SoV) is a familiar face in PR metrics, and share of search (SoS) is its sibling – more straightforward and based on searches, making it a reliable standard. Calculating your SoS? Free tools like *Google Trends* or features in paid tools like *Ahrefs Keyword Explorer.*

Remember, quality trumps quantity, so shout about the quality and relevance of your PR coverage, not just the sheer volume. Metrics like sentiment and engagement spill the beans on the real value of your PR hustle. Focus on the traffic that matters, conversions and engagement, to prove your PR campaigns pack a punch. Sync up with the brand's goals for insights that count.

8.2 Quantity vs Quality

Written by: Lauren Henley

Ever experienced that thrill of pitching a campaign, only to wake up the next day and discover a trove of links or media coverage? It's a feeling many chase in their digital PR pursuits. Going viral or hitting a specific link count often takes centre stage as a core goal, yet when probed about the 'why', explanations can be elusive.

Sure, a target link number can serve as a convenient KPI, but is it really the best measure of effectiveness? When it comes to digital PR strategies, the quest for both quality and quantity of links is something we hear daily.

Quantity vs Quality

In collaboration with *PR Week*, we conducted a survey, delving into the metrics PR professionals use to gauge the impact of their campaigns. Findings revealed that the majority (71%) identified the volume of coverage as their primary measurement metric. This was an outcome which, though not unexpected, carries its own set of implications. While the prevalence of this metric is noteworthy, it underscores a persistent trend. The industry's fixation on sheer numbers — be it links or coverage — often overshadows the crucial factors of quality and relevance. Anecdotal experiences further highlight the ramifications; instances where losing out on pitches occurred because projected link numbers fell short in comparison to competitors. Yet, it's imperative to foster a collective recognition that quantity doesn't always translate to value. Engaging in a race to the bottom, where the emphasis on numbers adds pressure to PR professionals, while diminishing the actual value delivered to clients, is a scenario we must collectively strive to avoid.

While there are hundreds of scenarios we see, these are four of the most common ones that crop up. Going through each of them, none rely solely on quantity to achieve the impact required. Creating briefs that focus on long-term success and KPIs that focus more on impact than outcomes, can help to drive the coverage that moves the needle.

In this chapter, we'll navigate through various scenarios, dissecting the delicate balance between the two and uncovering the nuances that make a difference...

Your Competitors Have Lots More Links than You	
Scenario	While benchmarking your backlink profile against your competitors, you realise that they have hundreds or thousands more backlinks than you currently have to your domain.
Assumption	You need thousands more links to compete and overtake your competitors.
Reality	Not all links are good links. A vast number of links doesn't necessarily indicate quality. Especially when, in so many sectors, companies are purchasing sponsored post links in huge numbers, which can lead to *Google* penalties.
Recommendation	Conduct a thorough backlink analysis on your domain and your competitors. Find any link gaps worth closing, and create a digital PR strategy that has your brand goals and target audience at the heart.
Quality or Quantity?	A balance of both.

You Have a Brand New Domain with No Links	
Scenario	You've launched a new brand with a fresh domain that has no links directed to it.
Assumption	You need to drive links to the domain very quickly to hit the ground running.
Reality	Building links without a clear brand voice or a technically sound website isn't going to move the needle. When good on-page content and a technically sound site are combined with links, it's like fuel on a fire.
Recommendation	Ensure you are in the best position to conduct digital PR before pursuing any link work. Whether undertaking DPR in-house or via an agency, you need to be sure who you want to target and why.
Quality or Quantity?	Quality.

You Have Lots of Toxic, Spammy Links	
Scenario	Due to either historic or recent poor link building practices, you have a large number of toxic links pointing to your site.
Assumption	You can drown out all of the bad links with lots of better ones.
Reality	Buying toxic links is often a reaction to a perceived deficit in a link profile. By flipping the script and pursuing more of those 'better' links in high volumes, this is also reactionary. Sometimes bad links go away on their own, but not always.
Recommendation	Consider your overall marketing goals and brand strategy. This should form the basis of a long-term digital PR plan. You can't put a number of links on condemning or recovering a domain, as a proper link landscape analysis should be conducted and acted upon to help build towards a better future.
Quality or Quantity?	Quality.

You Operate in a Highly Competitive Industry	
Scenario	The industry you operate in is very competitive and there are lots of different brands in contention for the top SERP spots.
Assumption	You need links to commercial pages and quickly. The best and easiest way to do this is by buying links to these pages to gain an advantage.
Reality	Buying links to a commercial page is a risky move. Buying links to your domain is against *Google*'s Webmaster Guidelines and is often an activity with diminishing returns. The worst-case scenario is you could get your key pages excluded from the SERPs entirely.
Recommendation	If you're selling a physical product, digital PR is a great way to drive placements and coverage to these pages without resorting to paid backlinks. There is also the additional benefit of campaigns that drive buzz on social media. If you sell a service, having great authoritative content on your commercial pages can make it easier for journalists to link to these pages and for digital PRs to create relevant content to get those links.
Quality or Quantity?	Both.

8.3 Share of Search

Written by: Andrew Holland

Share of search is a leading marketing measurement metric developed by marketers Les Binet and James Hankins. And, it's something that all marketers should be aware of. But what is it?

Share of search is an output metric. Essentially, you gather all the brands you compete against, combine the search volume for all the brands over a period of time, and then award each brand with their brand search share percentage. That is your share of search. OK, that's fine, but why should you care? People search for brands they are interested in buying from or have already purchased from. And this acts as a proxy for a brand's share of the market.

OK, so that is a lot of big words and big phrases. So, I'm going to break this down...

Leading vs Lagging Marketing Metrics

If you're reading this, it's because you're a marketing professional and want to learn how digital PR can help your business. This is key because there is no point in doing digital PR if it doesn't help support your growth. Part of this process is measuring its impact on your brand's performance. You see, digital PR impacts two types of metrics — leading and lagging. Leading marketing indicators attempt to predict the future, while lagging indicators predict the past. And lagging metrics are what most SEO reports are made up of.

When you look at your search console data or *Google Analytics,* you see the results of work done in the past, impacting today. Often, past advertising and SEO work undertaken is now coming to fruition. This lagging metric is why many SEO agencies see contracts cancelled: the impact of the work hasn't been fed into the data that businesses care about yet. You'll have a business asking, "Where are my sales?". But the issue is that the SEO work hasn't come to fruition yet, and this is going to become visible in the future.

Leading marketing indicators predict future likely business conditions. This is where share of search comes in. If you have a higher share of search, it indicates that you have a higher market share, and are likely to see an increase in sales in the future. But you might think, doesn't my search data predict the future? In reality, your search console and analytics data will contain lagging data from your SEO work — and also some leading data. For example, you might see increased traffic to product and category pages caused by SEO work done a few months ago. But the people discovering your business for the first time might not turn into buyers for many weeks or months.

You can already see what a challenging situation this is for business owners and marketing managers. On one hand, you are surrounded by data, but equally, it lacks context.

So, let's add some...

Share of Search: The Metric of Context

The share of search your brand has matters, because it will tell you how well your marketing is cutting through. Let's say you compare yourself with five brands competing with you in your space. If your share of search is increasing, it shows that your marketing is resonating with people, and they are searching for you.

If it decreases, it shows that either one of three things is happening:

1. Your competition is either spending more on marketing.
2. Your competition has more effective marketing than you.
3. Your marketing is not working.

The other thing worth considering with share of search is, as you compare yourself with others, you can see how market conditions affect your competition. If your search volume is reducing, is this the same for the others?

Regarding share of search, you need to be clear on this one fact. We are talking about brand search here. These are all the searches **around** your brand. Not just **for** your brand. But what about non-brand search?

Share of Buyer Intent Search

When a search is made, a person will search for a brand directly or enter a keyword into the search engine, where several brands will appear based on their optimisation. When Les Binet and James Hankins created share of search, this was not a part of it. They were focused on measuring brand performance. However, share of search equally applies to buyer intent search, where the brand is not searched for. This is where SEO and digital PR come into play.

When a consumer heads to search engines and is undecided on which brand to purchase from, they use keywords. These are what we call buyer 'intent search terms'. And just like share of search works for brands, your share of search for

SEO directly reflects the likelihood of being chosen by a buyer. In other words, you want to have a higher share of buyer intent search than your competition, as this increases the likelihood that someone will buy from your business.

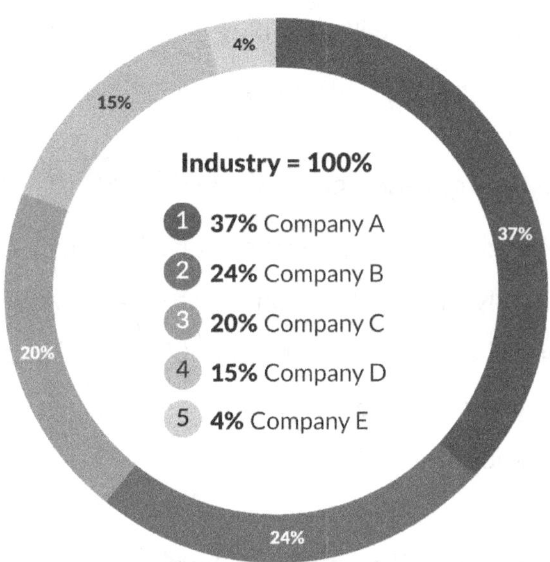

How to Measure Share of Search

There is quite a bit of data online about how to measure share of search. Essentially, you can do it for free using *Google Trends*. However, a few emerging tools make this far easier and more accurate — one such tool is called *MyTelescope*. But what about buyer intent, share of search? When you are looking at buyer intent share of search, you can use tools such as *Semrush* or *Ahrefs*, and you'll be able to see how much buyer intent search traffic you're gaining.

A word of caution, as you will need to examine this more closely than pressing a few buttons in a search tool. Many search tools will pull in all the traffic that a brand gains, some of which will be blog content that is purely educational and lacks meaningful value.

How to Use Share of Search for Your Marketing

So, we've given a whistle-stop tour of share of search, and it's probably time we told you how to use it. Share of search, both brand and buyer intent, should be used as a metric to inform business owners and marketing managers of brands' performance in search.

So, for example: if you have a high share of buyer intent search, but a low share of brand search, it's clear that while people buy from you, they aren't searching for you. This means you're vulnerable as you rely on organic or paid search channels. An answer to this would be to start to invest in brand marketing and publicity.

Equally, having a low share of buyer intent search might indicate that you are too reliant on acquiring customers from paid search. Or, that other brands are starting to acquire more customers with a larger share of buyer intent search. The point is that share of search gives you context to the data. By comparing yourself with others in your category, you can look at your marketing channels and how they are cutting through the noise and, more importantly, into consumers' buying decisions.

A Word on Brand Growth

Brands grow through sales, and sales come when two factors are increased: mental availability and physical availability. This is the likelihood that you will be thought of in a buying situation and the ease with which a person can buy from you.

When you increase your share of brand search and also your share of buyer search, you increase both factors. More people search for you, and also more people can find you via non-brand buyer intent search terms. And this is, again, another reason that digital PR serves as fuel for both. Being featured in the media exposes your brand to more people, fuelling brand search. Also, the links and mentions you gain fuel your website's authority, increasing rankings in the process.

8.4 Digital PR and ROI

Written by: Lauren Henley

So, why exactly do we do digital PR and outreach? Is it all about SEO, link juice, or boosting DA and referring domains? Well, while metrics like domain authority or domain rating do matter, the heart of any digital PR campaign isn't just about securing links. There are plenty of outcomes, ranging from increased sales to gaining coverage on a dream publication.

Every business invests in marketing activity with the expectation of a meaningful return. However, without clearly defined goals and aims, digital PR can leave you wondering whether you have made the right investment.

For a long time, brand-building marketing tactics have struggled to quantify its ROI. However, now in the digital age, while it's still not easy, it's simpler to assign value to work you've completed.

Based on the shared goals and aims you have for digital PR, there are different ways to assess the value you've added:

Goal: Boost Sales or Revenue of Your Brand or Client's Key Products or Services.

Working with a specific product or service, you have a distinct advantage in return on investment (ROI). This is, as long as you're ensuring that your campaign and coverage are precisely tailored to the intended audience.

By strategically tagging launch dates and key coverage dates in your analytics, you can seamlessly link these elements and establish a direct correlation with the increased sales of the product you are promoting. This data not only provides a means to gauge the effectiveness of your efforts, but also offers valuable insights into the specific types of coverage, channels, or publications that generate the highest interest in your brand.

Goal: Drive More Traffic to Your Website While Also Improving Rankings for Important Terms.

In navigating your website, it becomes important to tailor your strategy towards boosting the commercial viability of specific pages. Focusing on the most commercially relevant pages that warrant improvement is essential for a targeted approach. Formulating a clear strategy involves a comprehensive analysis of your website, delving into the competitive landscape, and tracking current media trends. Through meticulous research, your strategy will come into sharper focus, guiding your efforts towards impactful outcomes.

To identify areas for growth, it is key to narrow down your focus to a curated list of target pages, each chosen for the opportunities it presents. This strategic approach facilitates the creation of highly relevant stories that resonate with your audience. Leveraging tools such as *Google Analytics* enables the tracking of increases in both organic and referral traffic to your website.

Meanwhile, employing rank trackers provides ongoing insights into your site's performance in the search engine results pages (SERPs). Benchmarking against not only your own progress, but also that of your closest competitors, is key for a comprehensive assessment.

The assessment involves scrutinising ranking improvements, evaluating the search volume for targeted keywords, and projecting the expected increase in traffic, all while considering your website's conversion rate. This analytical process lays the groundwork for the creation of a formula to attribute return on investment (ROI), ensuring a strategic and measurable approach to your digital PR activity.

Goal: More Impressions, Branded Search Volume and Social Media Shares From Coverage and Placements.

Using various tools and techniques is key to evaluating the impact of your efforts. Leverage search engines, social media platforms, *Google Alerts*, and dedicated media monitoring tools to locate and scrutinise your published articles. A thorough analysis of metrics such as traffic, domain authority, and impressions will give you valuable insights. Track your social media followers by comparing the numbers before and after the digital PR campaign. Gauge the success of your campaign by measuring sentiment, engagement levels, comments, and shares related to your brand across various platforms. Tools like *Ahrefs*, *Coverage Book* or *BuzzSumo* can provide this information.

Delving into metrics like share of search (SoS) provides an insight into the increase in brand awareness. Over time, SoS serves as a reliable indicator of the online visibility and search demand for a brand, positioning it against its competitors. While share of voice (SoV) is a recognisable metric in public relations, share of search is a similar concept.

However, given the multiple versions and approaches to SoV, share of search offers a clearer and more standardised perspective. Calculating SoS is made accessible through free tools like *Google Trends* or integrated functions in paid tools such as *Ahrefs Keyword Explorer*. Additionally, tools like *My Telescope* streamline the process by automatically generating SoS reports, alleviating some of the manual workload associated with these assessments.

Goal: Secure Placements in Publications That Are Key to Endorsing Your Brand's Expertise and Are Consumed by Your Audience.

Understanding your clients' dream media placements is fundamental. We always ask about the publications they envision being featured in and the reasons behind these choices. However, it's crucial to acknowledge that securing coverage in these prestigious publications often presents a challenge. The allure of these dream publications lies in their prestige and stringent editorial policies, but it also comes with a hefty advertising cost. This makes it apparent that gaining coverage naturally, through a digital PR campaign, is not only a significant achievement but also saves money.

Demonstrating the value of such a campaign is straightforward when you consider the cost implications. By researching the expenses associated with placing an advertisement or collaborating on a sponsored article within these renowned publications, you can draw a meaningful comparison. This involves weighing the costs against the production expenses incurred for the carefully curated pitch that led to the acquired coverage — a figure typically substantially lower than the advertising cost.

Goal: Improve the Online Reputation of Your Brand.

Before commencing any reputation management efforts, it is important to address or resolve the underlying issues that led to negative coverage. In the short term, an effective way to gauge the positive impact on reputation repair is by conducting social sentiment analysis and evaluating recent brand coverage. These results can then be compared against the baseline figures obtained before the initiation of the campaign.

For more prominent brands, consumer research firms like *YouGov* frequently publish rankings indicating the brand's public perception. Over an extended period, the assessment can extend to sales and revenue data from *Google Analytics* or the company's sales records, offering insights into the recovery of revenue throughout the reputation management initiative. This allows you to assign a monetary value, demonstrating the return on investment (ROI).

Conclusion

Written by: Jane Hunt

As the world of SEO is ever-evolving, I expect digital PR to evolve with it. This doesn't mean to say that the tactics mentioned in this book won't be relevant in five to ten years. But instead, as competition for backlinks grows, anyone conducting digital PR activity will have to be very savvy and innovative to build good quality links at scale.

Not only are more SEO agencies and freelancers offering digital PR (at varying qualities) than ever before, making it more competitive than ever. Combine that with there being fewer journalists generally, and you really have to be on your game to earn those links.

Let's also not forget AI, too. If you're evolving your digital PR skills, you'll be investigating how AI can make your activity more effective, whether used for ideation, content creation, or outreach. But AI is not THE silver bullet — it still needs human expertise to power it, without that, there is no strategy which underpins the success of digital PR.

The brands that thrive, will be those that invest in digital PR, and that understand the value of it. Not just for SEO, but also for the impact it can have on driving brand awareness, and building credibility and trust with journalists, audiences, and *Google.*

Essentially, this is your playbook to devise the right strategy and tactics to deliver winning digital PR activity. Not only will it help you build good quality links, but it should also improve rankings and power brand growth.

The PR Dictionary

A

Affiliate Links — A unique link assigned to an affiliate partner by a company or brand. If someone clicks on this link and makes a purchase, the person who shared the link earns a commission or referral fee.

***Ahrefs* URL Rating** — The metric that evaluates the strength of a URL's backlink profile.

B

Backlinks — This is a link from one website to another, which indicates relevance and authority in the context of Search Engine Optimisation (SEO).

Brand Impact — Refers to the influence and perception a brand has on its consumers. It can be crucial in affecting their buying decisions and loyalty.

C

Content Marketing — A strategy focused on creating and sharing valuable and relevant content, to attract and engage a target audience.

D

Digital PR — Digital PR is the intersection of traditional PR, content marketing, and SEO. We're borrowing from traditional PR and content marketing techniques, and fusing them with SEO strategy to build organic search visibility and drive brand credibility and trust.

Domain Authority — A metric developed by *Moz*, which predicts a website's ranking potential on (SERPs).

Domain Rating — A metric used to assess the overall power and authority of a domain in the context of Search Engine Optimisation (SEO).

E

Experience, Expertise, Authority, and Trustworthiness (E.E.A.T) — A set of criteria used by Google's search quality raters to evaluate the quality of web content.

F

Feature Pitching — The process of proposing a story idea or article to media outlets to secure coverage for a brand, product, or individual.

Follow links — Also referred to as do-follow links, follow links are hyperlinks that allow search engines to pass authority and ranking value from one webpage to another.

G

Guest Posting — This is when someone writes and publishes content on a website they don't own, usually including a link back to their own site.

H

Hero Campaign — A longer, pre-planned piece of content that leverages creativity, strategic planning, and a thorough brand understanding. The goal is to captivate attention, achieve brand goals and secure links. It is often heavily backed by data and utilises copy and design to tell the story.

I

International Outreach — The process of pitching content to connect, engage, and collaborate with stakeholders, audiences, or communities across national borders.

J

K

Key Performance Indicators (KPIs) — Quantifiable metrics used to evaluate the success of a project or company in achieving specific objectives.

L

Link Building — The strategic process of acquiring hyperlinks from other websites to your own.

Link Juice — This is the authority passed from one webpage to another through hyperlinks, impacting search rankings and visibility - it is also referred to as link equity.

Link Reclamation — The process of finding and fixing broken or lost backlinks to a website. This involves finding websites that have mentioned your site but linked to an incorrect URL, and reaching out to those sites to add the correct link.

Link Spam — The practice of creating excessive or low-quality backlinks to a website, to try to manipulate search engine rankings. These links are usually irrelevant, unnatural, and come from sources with little authority and credibility.

M

Majestic Trust Flow — A metric developed by *Majestic* to assess the quality and trustworthiness of a website's backlink profile.

***Moz* Page Authority (PA)** — A metric developed by *Moz* to predict how well a webpage is likely to rank on SERPs.

N

Newsjacking — When a PR piggybacks on a current or trending news story to add a brand to the conversation, using expert comments, opinions, data, or quotes.

Nofollow Links — Hyperlinks with a 'nofollow' tag, which instruct search engines not to follow or pass authority from one webpage to another.

O

Organic Search — The unpaid, naturally occurring results that appear on search engine results pages in response to a user's query.

Organic Traffic — This refers to the website visitors who arrive at a site through unpaid, natural search engine results.

P

Private Blog Networks — These are groups of websites created solely to link to a single target website, often used to manipulate search engine rankings.

Proactive Content — Refers to planned and strategic content to achieve specific PR goals.

Product PR — Products are strategically placed into online content to promote a client's product.

Q

R

Reactive Content — Timely and responsive content created in response to current events and trending topics. Its purpose is to engage audiences by offering relevant and timely information and perspectives on the immediacy of a topic's popularity.

Referring Domains — These are websites that contain links pointing to a specific website, indicating external sources of backlinks.

Referral Traffic — Website visits that come from external sources other than search engines. This can include links from other websites or social media platforms.

Return on Investment (ROI) — This is a financial metric used to evaluate the profitability of an investment in relation to its cost.

S

Search Impact — This is the influence of changes in search algorithms or website optimisations on a site's visibility and traffic from search engines.

Search Rankings — These are the positions at which a website appears in SERPs for specific keywords or phrases.

Search Engine Optimisation (SEO) — This is the practice of optimising a website to boost its visibility and ranking in search engine results, thereby increasing organic (non-paid) traffic to the site.

Search Engine Results Pages (SERPS) — These are the pages provided by search engines in response to a user's query. They show a list of relevant websites, images, videos, or other content that is related to the search term.

Share of Search (SoS) — This metric is used in marketing to measure a brand's visibility and competitiveness in search engines. It is the volume of search queries for a brand as a proportion of all the search queries for all the brands defining a category.

Share of Voice (SoV) — A metric that shows a brand's visibility in a market or media channel, in comparison to its competitors.

Syndication Links — These are links that are distributed across multiple websites, as a result of a piece of content being published across multiple sites or platforms, broadening reach and visibility.

T

Traditional PR — Managing the reputation and promotion of a client's brand and products through traditional media channels such as newspapers, magazines, television, and radio, to create a positive image and reach a broader audience.

Traffic Flow — This refers to the flow of visitors or prospective customers across different online platforms toward a particular destination, like your website.

U

Unlinked Brand Mentions — These are online mentions (citations) of your brand, or anything directly related to your brand, which do not link back to your site.

V

W

X

Y

The Authors and Contributors

Authors:

Jane Hunt, Co-Founder and CEO — With a background in content marketing, building a digital PR agency seemed like the perfect fit. But Jane didn't want to stop there, she wanted to build one of the best digital PR agencies in the world. Ten years later, JBH has built a reputation for delivering best-in class digital PR campaigns with a focus on performance.

Rebecca Moss, Digital PR Director — Rebecca has 10+ years experience in SEO, content marketing, and link building. Over her five years at JBH, she's overseen digital PR campaigns for clients in the lifestyle, personal finance, and direct to consumer sectors. Rebecca also helps JBH grow, by utilising her knowledge to train the digital PR specialists.

Andrew Holland, Director of SEO — Andrew heads up the SEO department at JBH and is the author of The Value of SEO. First learning SEO while working in the police, Andrew later launched his own successful agency. He specialises in helping people to drive meaningful business results from SEO and has spoken multiple times at Brighton SEO.

James Renhard, Group Account Director — James has worked in Media and Marketing for 20+ years, including a background in journalism. He's an industry speaker, and former WPP, who has worked with a large variety of brands. His role includes working with clients to understand their needs, objectives, and expectations, ensuring JBH delivers exceptional service.

Sophie Clinton, Digital PR Manager — Starting out her career as a journalist, Sophie then moved to an in-house traditional PR role, before finally specialising in digital PR and link building. She is a knowledgeable PR manager at JBH, renowned for her ability to achieve award-winning results.

Abigail Fairfoull, Digital PR Manager — Abigail works alongside a growing PR and SEO team to drive brand awareness and engagement for a number of different brands across both B2B and B2C sectors at JBH.

Lauren Wilden — Lauren boasts over 10 years experience in digital agencies, working on PR campaigns for B2B and B2C brands.

Lauren Henley — With over 10 years experience in marketing, specialising in SEO and PR, Lauren ensures campaigns deliver benefits to businesses in both the short and long term.

Contributors:

Marketing:

Greta Andrejevaite

Copywriting:

Samantha Wright

Georgie Clark

Graphic Design:

Archie Da Costa

Rosie Venables

JBH
www.jbh.co.uk

www.ingramcontent.com/pod-product-compliance
Lightning Source LLC
Chambersburg PA
CBHW071606030726
47593CB00001BA/339